Flying Monkeys and the PRINCESS

KAREN KELLOCK PH.D.

**Manual for
Superior Men**

A complete theory based on Einstein physics, Political Psychology, Systems Theory and Archetypal Psychiatry.

FORMULA
All success attraction
All disease obstruction
All recovery elimination

You must fast on all three

OBSTRUCTIONS:
People
Habit
Food

Flying Monkeys and the Princess

Women don't do fighting themselves they get flying monkeys while looking innocent. I have a child's sensitivity and they incited riots against me. Nice aunt got a lawyer to torment me on a sadistic spree. Sweet sister started hot rumors all over town/I coulda been killed God. Once she reduced me to a stammering grasshopper she said "see, she's inferior".   Women make the best prison guards: tho' sweet little ladies in pics they are the most sadistic I heard.

Flying Monkeys and the
PRINCESS

EVOLUTION OF A LIFE
ELDERING THEN DEATH
NEVER RELATIZE CUSTOMS
DON'T FALL BACK INTO YOUR BAG
FEMALE ANGER AND GOSSIP
POWER FROM WITHHOLDING
JEZEBEL IS DANGEROUS
JEZEBEL TURNS EM AGAINST YOU
ESTABLISHING THE REAL YOU
SEX SEX AND MORE SEX
AFFAIRS WITH NEIGHBOR LADIES
NO-WALLS LIBERAL SOCIALS
FACE THE END
GRASSROOTS PARENT MOVEMENT
SOCIAL INDEPENDENCE
ADVERSARIAL JEZEELS
INCITING RIOTS LOOKING INNOCENT
BOUNDARY AND MORAL COLLAPSE
CONTROL THRU GOSSIP
HOME IS ALL—GUARD IT
DON'T ENVY SOCIALITES
AGING AND SAGING
ADDITION BY SUBTRACTION
SHOOTING AT SHADOWS IN THE HUMAN JUNGLE
THOSE SINNING ARE UNFORGIVING
DEPERSONALIZATION AFTER TRAUMA

Flying Monkeys and the **PRINCESS**

Flying Monkeys and the **PRINCESS**

Flying Monkeys and the PRINCESS

Preface to Flying Monkeys

EVOLUTION OF A LIFE

My life can be explained thusly: In order to come up you must first fall down and it's embarrassing.

Cinderella Syndrome hurt me badly. I have a child's sensitivity and they incited riots against me.

Women like that don't do fighting themselves they get monkeys to do it while looking innocent.

Sweet little aunt was so nice but got lawyer to be a bear chasing me up a tree/psychic violence.

Sweet sister was so helpful but started incendiary rumors all over town/I coulda been killed God.

Once she reduced me to a psychotic stammering grasshopper she said "see, she's inferior".

I'm so sorry to tell ya this about women but better keep em on your good side or hell's a-comin'

Women made the best prison guards. Tho' sweet ladies in pics they were the most sadistic I heard.

They were mean because they were primed by Jezebel & brainwashed by the liberal narrative.

FLYING MONKEYS AND THE PRINCESS

I was fine when alone with husband but open to society I caved into the undertow of the dumbed.

ELDERING THEN DEATH

My greatest achievement is a fence between me and those telling me what to think like a dunce.

They take your desire to be alone as rejection. Don't let em—going solo is your sacred right friend.

So goodbye, on the other side of here is death. Enjoy independence until your dying breath.

It's what your mind does to protect you. You don't feel anything, no pain, fear nor dread too.

I didn't have the guts nor temerity to say "I wanna be alone" and cuza that I was dethroned.

Just wake up to it, that's all. I've done things too where I didn't wake up til years later--the gall!

If you wanna be alone then INSIST you be alone/feel obviously PAINED when your privacy is gone.

Cuz people will ruin your life out of their own emptiness. It's a sucking spirit taking everything sis.

They're hoarders or messers so they escape the sewage by over-staying your tidy pad of niceness.

You would actually get people against me then bring them by. What a sick female and spy.

NEVER RELATIZE CUSTOMS

Never relativize customs saying it's all same cuz when it comes to human rights it's sadism.

FLYING MONKEYS AND THE PRINCESS

It's amazing how far you've come in a short time. That's God, full speed ahead after being dry.

"No man knows my history"--they don't have to know where you've been. Start fresh, new again.

Once reducing them to their abject state they could point to them and say "see, inferior rate".

Over the hill or at the top of your game? Don't let em rain on your parade cuz you're mid aged.

Trigger warning--before Bonanza and Gunsmoke, are they kidding? Suddenly it's all gone crazy.

Big companies blow woke smoke to cover up topics they don't wanna talk about, what jokes.

My overexcitability [OE] in trauma shot me into a new creative realm and boiled a new identity.

If you don't have the OE [overexcitability] you can't transmute energy from gross to gold.

If you don't have the OE [overexcitability] you can't make gold from [gross] transmuted energy.

You gotta be that crazy madwoman they all say you are to transform your energy from gross to gold.

DON'T FALL BACK INTO YOUR BAG

Every time you fall back into your bag [crutch, addiction, sin] you gotta start all over again. Repent.

Unless they're sweet ladies I really can't stand em. This modern woman is twisted/callous/dumbed.

There is no time nor space [Einstein]. So why couldn't God remove the stain-- sins erased?

FLYING MONKEYS AND THE PRINCESS

Instead of five back ten up, it was 1000 back and 2000 up--wild vacillations and extremes nonstop.

The extremes came from involvement with people. When alone with husband, high as a steeple.

They hurt me more by what they didn't say. 85% of communication is NONVERBAL ok.

Some people are so sensitive they belong in a monastery, that's how powerful it is see.

I suppose I was angry at men not knowing what's wrong and misplacing blame like the femmes.

Poor guys are so kind and gentle now, terrified of feminist anger or the rage of a mother.

FEMALE ANGER AND GOSSIP

Female anger is a loose canon. They become warriors with minds of steel traps copying men.

Yah she can't beat me up but she can get her Johns to do it and they are much crueler too.

When it comes to divorce courts and divvying up finances they can be most dishonest.

They get underhanded, making secret calls for lopsided deals showing power/strutting their stuff.

In "Everyone Loves Raymond" he's terrified of his wife. Most popular show for years, wonder why.

When they start to get revenge it feels so good they turn up the heat in return for past centuries.

Bad women rule thru gossip. They get on the horn and hold court negotiating/deciding wazzup.

FLYING MONKEYS AND THE PRINCESS

Ok if you wanna go to what's her name go ahead and go. I'll make it easy for you too you so and so.

I don't pay prostitutes to come over, I pay them to leave. Human Behaviorist Hugh Grant

She's the victim of the Cinderella Syndrome of two hateful sisters and a mother vs. her alone.

The hateful angry sisters & mother collude together as is always expected of birds of a feather.

A feminist wife's anger unhinged is the ugliest thing as she lets loose and vents her hellish yelling.

I didn't think I had it in me to act that way. Facing the past is facing demons but it'll all be ok.

POWER FROM WITHHOLDING

The weakest female has power over you if she has something you want. It's not about strength!

If one's speech reflects obsession with genitals it indicates masturbatory tendencies ya know.

Every sin leaves compensation in the moment. What we do reflects out so be careful/have caution.

If you're in deep sin be extra careful what you say cuz it reflects out in concentric circles ok.

One indication of sin is guarded behavior but that also is compensation and human nature.

It takes a lifetime. Seeing what works best, improving that. Seeing what doesn't, learning quick.

Acting sweet to your face. But being on the out list they incite hatred against you in any case.

FLYING MONKEYS AND THE PRINCESS

JEZEBEL IS DANGEROUS

I only learned these precious life lessons in a small liberal town or dysfunctional family system.

First they peg you and it's confirmed thru the grapevine then they fill their cup with it, bonafide.

The biggest problem is they think you're rejecting em just cuz you want privacy, oh hum.

She's dangerous cuz her friend are dangerous and she sics em after you when feeling jealous.

She's dangerous cuz her brothers believe her rantings when down in the dumps and envious.

The camp survivor couldn't trust because she saw how people can turn on you very viciously.

I had been sheltered in a conservative orderly home then war happened/to the wolves I was thrown.

I didn't see what you did to me until a decade later. That's always how it is with PTSD I hear.

Being imposed on/eclipsed is a major basis for mental illness--we'd be well if left to ourselves.

His sadistic cruelty busting all boundaries put me in denial quickly, an emotional coma see.

JEZEBEL TURNS EM AGAINST YOU

The dangerously insecure female primed him on the way so when he got here he was a bear.

You realize things later. Like your aunt always acting innocent after inciting riots earlier.

FLYING MONKEYS AND THE PRINCESS

She incited lawyers, neighbors, family members and strangers against me but oh-so sweetly.

What to do, yell at a gravestone or someone in a rest home? Eventually we gotta let things go.

The dangerously insecure female primed him on the way so he arrived here boiling angry.

Especially if she has high SMV [Sexual Market Value] he'll believe what she says about you.

ESTABLISHING THE REAL YOU

Eventually it's tiring keeping up a false front. And pointless, it's more profitable to be your self.

Lord take everything outa me that is not of You, that is of this world, a ball of mud of Elmer Fudds.

Read between the lines. You have the meaning of things then you have the virtue signaling.

They believed her as the old aunt but not you cuz you were young, creative and eccentric.

I'm not gonna lie to you, think what you want. To my best recollection I've presented myself.

Stay away from that system and you're essentially fine. It's just a buncha cobwebs and lines.

It's all old history like a dusty movie, eradicated immediately by relocating swiftly.

Re-invent yourself by getting free of the system that defines/frames you in that context.

When I told med school I was a vessel they didn't take me seriously after that/I lost my grant.

SEX SEX AND MORE SEX

Her idea of the good life is apparently promiscuous sex, drugs like meth and keeping house.

This is the dark side/modern Sodom and Gomorrah, involving all age groups in America.

Not just heterosexually promiscuous but invited to gay orgies in the district, that's the new Ms.

Every town has one: The Slut who's spirit is united with every man in town whom she owns.

They refuse to judge gays then push gay sex, then try it once and are hooked and hexed.

The sexual libertine is a proud bisexual too. It's just like Berlin before it all went to hell in WWII.

She can never be happy with a beautiful home cuz she's filled with demons from Johns.

It's disgusting, fifty year old women and their wet T-shirt contests or twerking in bars.

AFFAIRS WITH NEIGHBOR LADIES

It's when a husband has to worry about her lesbianism on top of her other loose ways, ok?

She called herself the "best BJ artist in town". Wonder why all the wives hated that old harridan.

Liberalism means ANYTHING goes. There are no lines to hold her bound as the lady falls.

It's a dark cavity, a bottomless cavern ready to swallow you up and totally untrustworthy on top.

FLYING MONKEYS AND THE PRINCESS

The "Best BJ Artist in Town" got herself a new house and car, that's how it is with the star.

The normal birds & bees perverts to this type of thing when even the old go sex crazy.

Behind a locked gate no one bothers me like Borrego Springs but that wrote 130 books see.

Let it all go cuz it's all gonna be gone anyway. Life changes and the acceleration is eery.

The more I was alone the more I felt imposed on when "they" came--the socials from town.

There is no bigger luxury in the world than a locked gate for inside is your home/destiny.

Outside the gate is hell--every culture shows this to a different degree, reflected architecturally.

NO-WALLS LIBERAL SOCIALS

Borrego had no walls but where I live now is ALL about walls: elaborate, high, basilic WALLS!

Without a locked gate people arrive unexpectedly then you lose autonomy adapting to fortuity.

Maybe cuz I'm Scotch this is obvious to me but in La Mesa and Borrego things were OPEN see.

There's walls everywhere here. It's reflected in their cultural psychology, it's an INNER journey.

People don't drop by here, but in Borrego they dropped by constantly: open society.

Country neighborhood: With boundaries/no social expectations I've never been more prolific.

The same person can thrive here but end up a dam scapegoat in a mental hospital there.

With each day it fades more from memory, the raw material for psych books: my desert journey.

I wanted to climb higher/transcend everyday culture but was blocked by the parochial for sure.

FACE THE END

If I'm always working I'm a dull girlboy and can't bring in success by my emptiness: fill me now.

FAST: day 1 have donuts/butter, 2 have tacos & salsa, 3 salad, 4 pizza & note how you suffer.

In other words with daily fasting each day's an accomplishment and then you select UP.

Vanity, vanity. It's gone, people die, they forget it, they're more important in their vision.

If tired take a nap. Let your life be catnaps and it's the life of great artists and thinkers: fact.

Could you feel nostalgia for a place of so much trouble? Yes, its perception reversals.

We live in a world where you can't trust a friend isn't sleeping with your husband? Are you kidding?

We live in a social climate where your best friend will turn you in just to have certain friends?

I got so used to treachery I expected it daily but it turns out it was just the hippies around me.

It was the human jungle and there was always something--eras of different treacheries.

FLYING MONKEYS AND THE PRINCESS

Eat once and then if you slip you'll do better tomorrow, that's it. Little by little you're perfect.

He has divided loyalties and teacher's pets. All kinds of things like that come from a narcissist.

Every time she arrived she ruined my life and it was always with others, monkeys in flight.

Leave them alone, they're in blue states and dumbed. Patriot or global, there's no middle ground.

GRASSROOTS PARENT MOVEMENT

We are seeing a grassroots parent movement to take back this country and it's wonderful to see.

We owe it to those people to know about the Holocaust but this generation is dumbed and lost.

They're even denying it ever happened. Can there be anything more callous and disgusting?

People were imposed on me by Kathy then Suzie 'til I learned my lesson about a locked gate see.

I wanted to look out to cosmic space with expanded mind then some hanger-on would arrive.

Living in a liberal social world for thirty years taught me more than a library of psych books.

SOCIAL INDEPENDENCE

I graduated to being all alone on my throne, away from the open social world you seem to own.

My entire day is my own, undistracted by people and events coming and going without a plan.

FLYING MONKEYS AND THE PRINCESS

I'm established. It took a lifetime to realize unique needs, what are they? INDEPENDENCE.

I'm not independent if having to talk to people I don't know or care to. The constant human zoo.

But she owns the town as The Slut and so I bow out, escaping to my solo destiny free of nuts.

My days are my own, her days are the towns who'll bring her down without boundaries drawn.

Established: not just in a nice house but impervious meaning you can never get to me now.

Enjoy your freedom from people/independence of uniqueness while you can/GUARD it man.

Fear being put in camps or other people in your houses. Cuz that's our future in their words.

ADVERSARIAL JEZEELS

Every time she came she brought an adversary who wanted to take from or insult the Ace.

They were your support group, what you knew. And suddenly they have turned against you.

To be treated as subhuman suddenly is very frightening whether it be in a small town or family.

Whether in a crowded station or all your friends stuffed in my living room, vamoose/be gone.

She fights thru flying monkeys, Johns enlisted as her personal army against enemies/jealousies.

I won cuz I got a locked gate and house protected from lush and louse with lights, guards, dogs.

FLYING MONKEYS AND THE PRINCESS

"We want to be together but we want to be alone more" said a happily married couple living apart.

Established: in a house on a hill too high for you to climb, safely sequestered from that old life.

When they turned as a group it was truly scary cuz i had no place to turn even the liberal church.

A liberal town is a herd that will turn suddenly and it's hard removing the stain slandered daily.

My persecutors weren't an invading army but people you saw as friendly so I prayed to God almighty.

INCITING RIOTS LOOKING INNOCENT

See that little old lady? She's really a scorpion how she incited riots against me from everybody.

As Psalms says it was **YOU** my trusted friend who turned on me and it terrified me truly.

You got your friends against me and they were **CRUEL** while you appeared innocent you witch.

What is he protecting you from: the **WORLD**. Women belong in the home with boys and girls.

For the world will insult and cajole you to go its way but a loving husband wants you unique ok.

The man protects the home while the woman creates this loving fortress in a world of danger/chaos.

The utter bliss of coming behind a wall where you all can't get to me anymore you blobs.

People and the outer world are horrible so get your own routines going, happy events so memorable.

FLYING MONKEYS AND THE PRINCESS

All I know is he's always there for me otherwise we're in our respective houses/offices happily.

Don't fear when slut or swindler flourishes like the olive tree cuz they'll be mowed down suddenly.

"I can't express the feeling of being dehumanized but it's primarily terror". Holocaust Survivor

You can be dehumanized by your own family who speak about you like you're not in the room.

You're own family can dehumanize you to strangers as they all hate you while gathered together.

If the victim allows it decompensation kicks in and he spirals down to totally vulnerable and fallen.

BOUNDARY AND MORAL COLLAPSE

The victim suffers both boundary and moral collapse, he's a non-person and an empty shell.

He was such a superior social manipulator they all believed the alcoholic husband against her.

She went from one man to another to protect her and just got increasingly worse characters.

Finally she caved in and questioned her own sanity, agreeing she was the problem maybe.

The townspeople went from being victims of social fascism to perpetrating it themselves.

The persecution gains a momentum of it's own and the frenemies enjoy doing it even on friends.

People come and go but God remains. Don't make em that important, rely on God to maintain.

FLYING MONKEYS AND THE PRINCESS

People come and go but God remains. Don't make em that important, rely on Him to maintain.

Let a concentration camp survivor tell you the right priorities in life. Think on that, see the light.

A concentration camp survivor wants a fence and a locked gate. Don't ever question that mate.

It felt like a roomful of people imposing on me. All yelling simultaneously as I went crazy.

The communist spirit manifests in a neighborhood when you refuse to rent rooms or want solitude.

The liberal socialist wants you to COMMUNE: chum up, bunk up and shack up but NO SOLITUDE.

CONTROL THRU GOSSIP

They're dam suspicious of anyone wanting to be alone and the wife gossips about him in Al-Anon.

She controlled me outa fear of what she'd say to people or Al-Anon. That's how she ruled everyone.

The alcoholic husband is doubly catty. That's how he puts her down and him up as Big Daddy.

These are BANDS of control between people that destroys lives making us crooked and old.

What's the worst thing about prison? CROWDS. In solitary you can at least have books.

I would not wanna go back to that, those hard lessons learned from the Ph.D. in the Streets, hurt.

Until you manage people/lay down boundaries your life will be a frenzy of users coming at thee.

Who'd wanna go back to that, hard lessons learned from the Ph.D. in the Streets and getting hurt?

Younger means you're still being tortured. Older = your Waterloo is over, enjoy fruits of labor.

A holocaust happens when we cross the lines of civility and then not care how others are treated.

He hurt me so much I wanted to die. What's he gonna do to me next I'd daily ask myself, no lie.

Narcissists have no empathy and that is the dividing line between civility and systemic tyranny.

Meeting your friends was a Nazi-like atmosphere that was downputting and insulting dear.

HOME IS ALL—GUARD IT

You can't trust all will be ok. If on a street without a fence you're up a creek without a chance.

Don't let home be a honey trap or it'll be your trap and you'll lose everything again: fact.

Keep users at bay or lose everything I say. No RV hookups, weekend stays or shack ups.

Don't fear being seen as selfish cuz you want solitude in your home. It's your castle/sanctuary, ohm!

Whoever comes in your home brings demons in with him and they all wanna hang around.

They didn't make a nice home for themselves or they don't have one at all so you're it that's all.

My home is my protection against the insults of your friends towards me so keep out please.

FLYING MONKEYS AND THE PRINCESS

Established: See need to relocate behind a locked gate cuz in a minute people change your fate.

They tormented me for years until I realized I don't have to take this and moved away, cheers.

I was so happy alone. You came with your angry guy and I was dethroned: a recurrent song.

If you're into meth, bad associations, affairs with married men you'd better get a fence then.

Even if you live a good clean civil honest life, better get a fence cuz they're coming for ya, aye.

DON'T ENVY SOCIALITES

Like a Jew in Nazi Germany they will hurt you on purpose because it's seen as patriotic.

Don't envy a socialite cuz she's in this fight and ultimately it means a useless life/blight.

Useful life: Loving those in your charge and creating a health giving environment, the home.

We're all gonna be dead soon so enjoy your life while you can. Have no jealousies/covet nothing.

For work expect justified remuneration [money] and recognition [that means you honey].

Silently looking out the window in quiet reverie--THAT is the most productive use of time see.

Established: Learned from bad fate, saw a reason to relocate, happily thriving behind a locked gate.

Established queen: finally knowing enough for a locked gate and a husband to protect your fate.

They laughed at me trapped in a syndrome. I was the laughing stock of everyone around.

I was shooting at shadows in the human jungle. I didn't know what the hell was going on.

I literally had to write these books to figure it out and i still don't know but I've overcome it all.

STOP little anchors to your prior identities: MEMORIES. Don't give em any energy.

Trying to adapt to the everyday mundane world yet my mind was way out there, enthralled.

STOP memories, the anchors to prior [lower] identities and now you have room for higher things.

Defocus from memory and new doors open. It's a pie budget in the brain not luck man.

Where's those villains Quinn and Bill? We don't like it when things are going so well.

AGING AND SAGING

There came a day when I wasn't offended [just saging] by mention of the life phases of aging.

S So you're ten/twenty years older--start taking naps and speaking your mind to brats.

Who would wanna maintain the ways of youth just to get approval from the popular groove?

Older you're the top of your game and you couldn't have risen to that peak any other way.

No one can do what I do and I'm totally peculiar too. i wasn't born that way, it's a lifelong brew.

FLYING MONKEYS AND THE PRINCESS

The degree of peculiarity of the human genotype equals the degree of sagacity, aye!

Every species has it's genotype and genius is ours. It needs only be developed after discovered.

Shut up guy. Maybe your wife doesn't want you to formulate into words what she's like.

To recover from narcissistic abuse is finally finding the self, disentangling it from ego hell.

Her illness was introjection of her mother's projected shadow resulting in lunacy from below.

The past is only a lower dimension [Einstein]. Don't give it any energy & now you'll make time.

It's like God put me in a caldron and boiled me for 30 years to produce the matrix by the Potter.

And when it was all done and I'd learned all my lessons He took me to my mansion of protection.

I love my country neighborhood, I've no desire to live in a fast city or fancy gated community.

ADDITION BY SUBTRACTION

The narcissist is paranoid, insecure and brainwashed by shame-based thinking/won't change.

If the thinking is deeply shame based they won't let you up after failing--there's no forgiveness.

Of course porn is cheating. He's looking at other women's bodies and many are teens.

As you pull away from him and his pathology you'll see the principal of addition by subtraction.

You subtract him and life shows addition but I'd say it increases exponentially by multiplication.

You're gonna add to your quality of life by subtracting the detractors and those time-wasters.

Anyone in the narcissist's world exists as their supply so they can feel better about themselves.

Rather than caving into specific resentments, see the past as an asylum you escaped from sis.

If you survived a war you wouldn't focus on specifics but just "the war" then try moving past it.

In a small town little things become big things very quickly: see it as a herd, delete memory.

SHOOTING AT SHADOWS IN THE HUMAN JUNGLE

See the past as chaos in the human jungle which in a small town becomes persecution, a jail.

A shame-based system won't let you forget it. They want you hurt forever with no forgiveness.

In small towns everyone knows everything and when you fall they all hop on the bandwagon.

TREACHERY: They can't understand how you could be so self-forgiving and move on casually.

Though Jesus forgives the payment is stiff in a small town with envy all around: relocate, now.

It's the Dunning-Kruger effect as the dumbed social controls the elect and I'm sick of this.

Even living out in desert wilderness you still gotta see them at the post office, I didn't like this.

My biggest accomplishment is not books/money but a locked gate protected from you honey.

It will hold you back trying to get em back. God'll get em better so just do your work/no slack.

It's the sex sinners who are biggest gossipers. It's all compensation for shame down under.

In that era of your past the herd was turned in a certain direction that's all, see it's a dumb mob.

THOSE SINNING ARE UNFORGIVING

The more they're secretly sinning the more they're entirely unforgiving of you, a sweetie.

No smart person can last too long in the throng without feeling something's wrong/exhaustion.

He's just another human with a dirty beard who says "fuckin" every other word, forget em girl.

The traumatic stress became so great I exploded as the energy reconstellated a new matrix.

It was my overexcitability [OE] that saved me as the huge reactive energy created a new Me.

With less OE I woulda caved in to the treachery with addiction, lassitude, withering solitude.

The trauma released a bomb inside as the scattered forces became a rod of iron bonafide.

[OE] everexcitability was a boiling caldron for making gold: a hero's alchemic transformation.

It takes what it takes for each to bring this energetic transformation to royalty from a freak.

FLYING MONKEYS AND THE PRINCESS

From scattered forces [confusion and crookedness] to a rod of iron as God's man, a fortress.

Their pride is a reaction to shame inside. Satan's other name is Arrogance and he's also snide.

DEPERSONALIZATION AFTER TRAUMA

The brain's stress response to trauma is fight-flight then depersonalization [self goes in coma].

Not knowing who I was anymore I couldn't stand up for myself, all boundaries busted/laid bare.

My cure for depersonalization was to be present for myself, new routines as the magic elf.

What/who was me? Home life, order, music, beauty, pets, thinking and writing: THIS was me.

What to do? What's right in front of you. Point by point the path is obvious in little things too.

The "I" became my routines, affections, aversions, controls and how I maintained my home.

The "I" was not what it was: my past, traditions, ancestral inclinations, society's narratives.

The "I" was so intensely subjective now that everyone who visited me became a dam imposition.

They didn't put their things away/maintain order or whatever, I had to be alone to be clever.

In this social era of blurry boundaries people will drive you crazy if you don't lay em down early.

Guests are like fish, after three days they smell. Being a proud Scot I'm independent as hell.

STOP SAYING YOU LOVE EVERYONE

Stop saying you love everybody. That's the biggest buncha bull I ever heard cuz you hate me.

Mental illness NOT inside job but being ECLIPSED by another where self disappears altogether.

I became their projections. I became what they said I was like some sick script I was reading out.

That's how the brain works, I can't help it. I became a robot, a nut. I had many crutches/ruts.

Overexcitability [OE]: with more things going on he's easily pushed over the line, confusion.

So the "I" became a series of routines to delimit confusion and disorder. Simplicity, order.

SAINTS SENSE SUPERFLUITY

The saints have always sensed superfluity in the lives or ordinary men. Unnecessary clutter/ruin.

The lives of saints shows renunciation of one complication after another. William James

Most of these complications are relations. If you confuse/deplete my energy then go man.

The saints have always sensed with disgust how the ordinary want approval, how they lust.

The saints have always known heaven is clean order and hell is dirty disorder, earthly junkers.

I want home like a library or monastery and if you are a messer/hoarder you can leave today.

FLYING MONKEYS AND THE PRINCESS

I dutifully did what God told me to do every day then He gave me much more to oversee ok.

I renunciated complication till there was no one left. Lonely at first but then I flourished, happiness.

My soul became so sensitive I had to abandon all conversation lest I get hurt. William James

Then when they fail to find a flaw they'll always pull the age card: society's approval is useless.

KEEP HOUSE WITH QUINTESSENTIALITY

I assign household duties while it is still dark. I run my home like a Swiss watch/a martinette.

Young maid sang insulting songs about her mistress to her face. Maintain your own place.

Make yourself as independent of people as you can then assemble your TEAM of like minds.

I have my quintessential clothes assembled ready to go and my diet squared. Simplicity is warrior.

Not the superfluity and non-essentiality of ordinary men but most important and nothing else.

You gotta have your best/most appropriate stuff ready and the rest gone, irrelevant/in the way.

You think you're so dam smart and clever, well I don't think you are and I got bored or whatever.

Preach your thing to fans but I'll ascend to God's plans and that's my new stable life, amen.

I know it hurts: embarrassment from what the devil did in you. He's gone but memories come thru.

FLYING MONKEYS AND THE PRINCESS

You were weak/the hedge was down so evil came flowing in/you were part of the crowd.

It wasn't you, it really WAS the devil who made you do it so we repent to stay strong/prevent it.

Now you're sweet, as gentle as a dolphin. But with high boundaries you also get rid of em.

With losers around your sensitive soul picked up their garbage and you mimicked the clowns.

KEEP YOUR OWN HOUSE [STABLE]

Realize it's the housekeeper you paid to keep order who's creating bedlam/you can't afford her.

I paid her to bring order as housekeeper but evil spirits in her destroyed me/I can't afford her.

Her Jezebel spirit was so strong I'd get into crying jags all day long and even wanted her to move in.

Her Jezebel spirit was so strong my husband landed in hospital with aneurisms from tension.

Her Jezebel spirit was so strong I'd get into crying jags all day long and even asked her to move in.

Her Jezebel spirit was so strong she appeared indispensable and I wanted to adopt.

The stress from trauma can so morph a person he can be cruel after being kind or visa versa.

I was so stressed out I relied on the inferior to get me thru it but they punished me as scapegoat.

Woulda saved myself years by staying alone and relying on God but no, I had to get involved.

FLYING MONKEYS AND THE PRINCESS

EVERY TIME I relied on people to protect me from someone else they turned out far worse.

Even details like getting up the same time each day took me outa my derealized state.

SCAPEGOAT SYSTEMS

As an unrecovered adult child of alcoholics she was never laughing but always cleaning.

The abuse is imbalance of power where the kids don't have a chance to get along together.

There's only one scapegoat as mom triangulates by pitting one against the other see.

The emotionally immature parent creates distance between siblings to prevent treachery.

In a feud the wife takes one child, dad takes the other and they spark rivalries lasting forever.

Insecure alcoholic mom kept complaining about kid sister to the big who deepened the rift.

The one not towing the line pretending all's ok is the target of the mother in denial obviously.

The one questioning the system is the one calling out the parents and the blatant injustice.

Mom said don't kiss anyone I didn't want to and then finally fired my trumpet teacher too.

When I wouldn't kiss my aunt she was so annoyed she'd gossip about me to girls/boys.

Some females have children, some are barren. When the officious ask me that's what I tell em.

Everyone loved Jolly Jimmy but he tortured his wife in private honey/the LIE drove her crazy.

IT'S A GREY WORLD

She had a problem but overcame it and is famous but you can't stand it can you Ms. Envious?

Just stating a different opinion can get you attacked. It's now a whole new world in fact.

Pugnacity is common even amongst women. Threatening violence is how they get er done.

Men took sexual advantage of her trauma bond and collapsed boundaries. They will pay.

You like it, that's all you gotta know about it. The. subconcious selects, it has perfect tact.

The others object to the saint's selections since it's all about the current narrative to them.

The saints always object to the silly fashions of the era they're in. They transcended it man.

Nobody does what I do/no one does what you do so focus on success/work in quiet certitude.

To work put on the music, take a toke and look out the window. Write what comes up/you know.

PREPARE FOR WAR

After WWII I ask: how could we be so lucky in this generation? Well we may not be soon.

Your checklist: I'm in a safe state, away from a street and with a fence and a locked gate.

FLYING MONKEYS AND THE PRINCESS

It's not enough your house looks good or the neighbors are fancy, you need SAFETY.

You don't want em to get to your door. You want a buffer zone too, inner fences and more.

You gotta get outa blue states where your life's an open book to the officious neighborhood.

I wanna country neighborhood where everyone minds their own business, in-grown in a sense.

CALIF: Where cops can extract you from your house and haul your sorry ass to mental health.

Rapidly changing demography is the major reason to relocate and don't apologize for it mate.

HOW WOMEN FIGHT

Flying monkeys fights: women jealous of each other get their sidekicks to punish the other.

De-Age: by sidestepping culture in the desert wilderness, I avoided the aging social chaos.

I feared her as a dangerous woman due to her violent flying monkeys while seeming innocent.

She was my worst persecutor always through her flying monkeys. Always come alone I now say.

What I went thru with the men in your life. They were mean to me cuz you primed em, aye.

I was scared of her tendency to triangulate against me. Underhandedness, treachery.

There was always secrecy. Underhanded triangulations with even strangers against me.

FLYING MONKEYS AND THE PRINCESS

If you're not smart enough to understand me you're gonna be imposing on me so stay away.

I don't give a dam what your friends/family say about me so keep it zipped or go away.

By the time a female claws her way to success she's so friggin' exhausted she don't feel blessed.

What was your biggest obstruction? Women and secondly men: the human element, amen.

Stop triangulating me with your family and friends. My relationship is to you: get some class.

LIFE'S A PIE

Since life's a pie you can't envision success if still working nor the future if always remorsin'.

It's all done tho' I'll be writing forever. It's what I do resolving contradictions or whatever.

A week vaca after writing out 63,000 proverbs for all of ya. Fast for two days and lotsa musica.

Two days lookin' out the window and letting the mind spin out unhindered by what I know.

I've gotta break the mold, change the matrix, give myself a break from all this sameness.

After completion of the Creative Act [being a vessel] we become a page again, pure/humble.

Retirement resembles infantilization, mysticism and a little psychosis. Now you can produce.

If you're one with your husband and he reads then your mind expands at the same rate see.

My goal: to become a child again. To stop this constant endless spoutin' and just be sunnin'

Gonna enjoy the fruits of my labor now. I deserve it cuz I did Thy work as You told me how.

Time will pass and I'll shrivel up and die. But these words go on and that is why I cried.

Nothing to worry about, the work is all done. Just look good and show up, now starts the fun.

FASTING INSIGHTS

You don't have to select a diet. Just do a one day fast and let your body naturally choose it.

After just one day fast junk food has an entirely different effect. It's like yuk/a headache.

The same inferior foods you could take before the fast will now make you sick as heck, alas.

If I have to **NOT-EAT** to get there I will **NOT-EAT** and get there I swear: it's the last tier.

You can also eat every other day or thrice a week. I like this method the best I think.

There's a third category of eating disorder [ED]: fasting food to prevent choking in sleep.

Phone charging/bath: Hookup at park to use their facilities not use me for these things lady.

ANOREXIC SYNDROME BE GONE

Once inside the anorexic syndrome it gains a life of it's own: you're trapped and all alone.

FLYING MONKEYS AND THE PRINCESS

We Scotch love our big breakfasts and as an ulcer victim that's when the nausea hits.

Food became all about what holds down inflammation not what's in it like anti-oxidants/vitamins.

I'd eat donuts broiled in butter if it would hold down inflammation like nausea from ulcer.

I found the trick for me: Eat a big breakfast then don't eat so the healing process proceeds.

We had our starchy, sugary, fatty, proteinrich breakfasts then we'd work all day refreshed.

We were so delighted after our ridiculous breakfasts--you can't get that with mere salads.

After all that it's not necessary to eat lunch nor dinner so just enjoy thy fast and be a winner.

Tho' well after years of such trauma I have something to show for it: an ulcer in the stomach.

EAT SO YOU CAN FAST

If buttered donuts for breakfast stops the pain so you can fast for the day, do it and be ok.

One can't work all day out in the fields by living on greens drinks but dense food of kings.

EAT then don't eat. Eat enough so you don't have to nor want to eat again: content and sweet.

They eat salads and fruit then binge all day long. No, eat dense and rich now fast/be strong.

Buttered donuts with pomegranate juice: that makes a great breakfast too now enjoy the view.

Fruit, beans, rice, corn. Man can live on glucose or fat and protein--his diet can endlessly morph.

Most females in my ancestry were celibate, single and childless [barren]--it's a very rare one.

Don't make plans for the entire project, move point by point as you see it. Like a battleship.

For God to bless America America must bless God but maybe He'll give us a reprieve like Nineveh.

KARENKELLOCK.ORG

My website is a spacescape, free of geography language culture just the universal see.

The picturestrips [discovery] run vertically then you have the world music chill station see.

Then you have the **BUY KK BOOKS** button for the 130 books by KK & how to buy them.

The picturestrips took a year each and the 130 books took ten years after 40 years of study.

They laughed at me cuza the path I had to take, not knowing a dam thing until it was late.

Higher poetic images [tweets] in Johanesse verse drawn from science, mythology, nature.

It's composed of 63,000 tweets in Johanesse/Science verse that were all presented here first.

All landmark discoveries in science were presented artistically and all had a general formulae.

All literary and science discoveries are presented in brutal reversals and corrective solution.

All literary and science discoveries are presented in brutal reversals and corrective solution.

Discovery changes the paradigm in science suddenly then it's proven by the mere tech guys.

The quips bring insight through subconscious analogies not by me telling em see.

The TEST of a discovery is: does it work? If insight is gained then we've removed the curse.

The barren female writer: I write 18 hours a day cuz it's the only legacy I'm leaving the earth.

CARICATURES OF MEANNESS

CARICATURES OF MEANNESS

CARICATURES OF MEANNESS

They become caricatures of meanness. It's enough to create biliousness so we truckle to stop this.

I couldn't criticize him for a thing or it was like I was declaring war on this toddler emotionally.

There's no creativity if all actions are reactions to him/her. It's like a grenade range for sure.

If no one protects you, you must do it yourself. Treat self like a vulnerable child/guard the elf.

See things THRU TIME. How he feels today is not how he'll feel tomorrow: don't give in/go blind.

I was attracted to dashing men who hurt me. Our psychology reverses with early trauma see.

EARLY TRAUMA CORRECTION

Our psychology seeks to correct the early trauma [of being rejected] by seeking bad outlets.

Tangents on the Hero's Path can be trying on friends and family but things calm down eventually.

They act, you react. They're Narcissus, you're Echo. You must stop this cycle to be successful.

I stayed no-contact for months and he'd lost his shine. It's all fake isn't it mom? Yes Lass, aye.

How to get more money: Always look good for your man--perfumed, decked out and lovely.

CARICATURE OF MEANNESS

Don't keep going back in time/lower levels in your mind. These old battles are mental binds.

You both were younger then and after all, you let him in. These are mental anchors friend.

MORE ENERGY, MORE SINNING

The most energetic become the biggest sinners. Change direction and they're biggest winners.

He thinks if he keeps you in the defensive mode, he wins. You can't ever relax in bedlam.

You can't reform these people. Maturity happens from inside out and it's a losing game with evil.

Don't let old grudges become mental anchors. The devil wants to waste your time my dear.

Let the flame dim then go out. Now, go full throttle by kicking him out and yourself up a notch.

Drop the illusion that you're the one who's gonna get thru to them. And by the way, avoid em.

They bare no criticism: it just means you don't like them--an automatic reaction of narcissism.

Not that they could change, or think of change or become self-aware, but a declaration of WAR.

HE'S NEVER GONNA CHANGE

He's gonna go on as he is and never change, except his symptoms get more bizarre with age.

His type will not give you deep connection nor can you look to him for direction so just move on.

CARICATURE OF MEANNESS

No thank you, the thrill is gone. You've done me in my fickle friend who's here today/soon forgotten.

You need him like a ten ton weight on your neck. Mark my words and progress/don't turn back.

SEASON OF TREASON

The biggest ageist is now a bag of wrinkles resembling nothing of his former self: karma is hell.

Don't take it no more and the rest is easy cuz then it's just yourself which is genius called crazy.

The period of punishment and season of treason were the same thing. The hedge was down see.

If you gotta good thing going don't mess it up. Don't have to learn from disaster or arrogance.

He wins by keeping you in hysteria. Just when things are peaceful, think what happens to ya'.

They're not just stupid, unreasonable and useless but DANGEROUS so avoid their chaos/circus.

HOW THE UNIVERSE WORKS

If one repents and stays high the transition period has great synchronicity and miracles see.

Magic coincidences--miracles--uncanny synchronicities: this is the cornucopia see.

The lower vibration is the dark consequences of sins: hateful principalities coming thru persons.

The higher life repels the bad and attracts the good to the WHOLE seed kernel: the True Self.

CARICATURE OF MEANNESS

The lower rung, the period of punishment/season of treason, is the path to beauty from ashes.

When I relapsed back into drinking the miracles suddenly stopped. Recovered lady drunk

Learning that I could not drink took decades of dung and dangerous escapades. Karen K.

The dark lower rungs are boundariless. With individuation and separation we protect ourselves.

The King's castle is surrounded by guards and gates, the homeless are victims of bad fates.

I was a trusting naive rudderless kid not a shrewd fox. It took decades of dung for Karen Kellock.

THE ALCOHOLIC CAN'T DRINK

Thinking he's captain of his own ship is the blinding delusion of the active alcoholic when lit.

Thinking he's still captain, with one beer he's demoted and loses all control: that was me ya' know.

The alki cannot drink alcohol and attempts at social drinking will always bring ruin eventually.

One beer and soon he's drinking all day/night and trying to get more. This is the disease forever.

Our affinities also change. At a certain point God yanked me from my tiny cabin to a mansion.

After I was sober, honest and decent the shack didn't match the person: good riddance, amen.

Liberal academics push social drinking for alcoholics. Their subjects die trying it has been noted.

CARICATURE OF MEANNESS

Just as the movie Wine and Roses, you can't predict where you'll end up after you can't stop.

I drank due to heartsickness, early trauma. It soothes those thoughts but then it surely turns on ya.

It's been 25 years now of happy sobriety and life is a continuous magic miracle I can safely say.

HERO'S PATH: EXPAND/CONTRACT

On the Hero's Path you must expand before you can contract--and that can be hellish in fact.

I had to experience many bad things to choose the right way and be adamant about it ok.

"Nothing astonishes people more than the truth." Mark Twain said that and he's beloved too.

I had to suffer invasion and hurt to be adamant about boundaries: before, I was very weaselly.

To be rigid steel about boundary details like it was part of my DNA: that's what i mean ok.

Don't let a man in your home when you're there alone and if it's a date make him take you out.

He must take you out/spend money not come to your home for a bootie call then leave honey.

Border's flooded for two years, why keep hearing about it. Repeat/fillers when we already know it.

She didn't know enough to slap the man's face. It all marks the moral & boundary collapse ok.

LIBERAL CONTRADICTIONS

CARICATURES OF MEANNESS

Like communism it's an all-consuming point of view that tolerates no argument/is adamant.

White men have been disarmed between the ears by a cult calling truth racist/a pervasive fear.

We lose rights to a nanny state cuz it takes tyranny to keep diversity from destroying itself see.

How can environmentalists encourage the importation of more people? Contradictions: liberal.

WHY CELEBRATE DIVERSITY?

Why should we celebrate diversity if it means our dwindling influence? It is obvious insanity.

California's bad ideas go national incredibly fast. If it goes down the rest follows like dominoes.

Faddish ideas from California are nurtured by the FEDS but Trump would surely trash em instead.

The FEDS actually find California's insane ideas very sexy and attractive. Can you believe that?

Good ideas like human development & flourishing are pushed out by bad ideas like reparations.

California shows Cloward and Piven: Overload the boat then it all explodes into communism.

Retirement is movies, music and musing. No more news rehashing: just get the headlines.

All day and night the superior man puts things into place. It's a trip to co-create with God ok.

KELLOCK PSYCH TEXTBOOKS FOR A LOST GENERATION

Flying Monkeys and the
PRINCESS

BETRAYAL IS CENTRAL IN PSALMS

Crime follows poverty cuz in lack people get grabby and greedy and easily bust boundaries.

Your own sisters sided against you and it was brutal. It's something you'll never forget too.

But read the Psalms and you'll see how CENTRAL betrayal is in the scheme of things.

The first paragraph: they GATHER TOGETHER to bring down God's own, the elect He's chosen.

Get over it. Joyce Meyers was raped 200 times by age ten by dad yet became a great evangelist.

Foremost in mind should be that your Father is kind and doesn't want you down on thine.

God doesn't want you hurt/upset anymore over what they said about you/why they hated you.

"They hated you before they hated Me" said Jesus. That's all you need to know your highness.

Stop cringing over memories that anchor you to prior identities when you were wasting away.

Let it go, let it ALL GO. Fasting assists you in this and when we die it's all meaningless you know.

It's who you are now, God doesn't see who you were then. He even defended you when in sin.

Let it go and forgive all. You've done bad stuff when under a spell or compensating for a fall.

THE. SOCIAL ERA VS. INDEPENDENCE

It hurts being pegged wrongly to buttress someone else's false identity as his strategy.

It's not enough to lock my door I wanna locked gate so they can't get that far: lessons of war.

Your independence signaled you were a nuisance or too big for your britches so they reacted.

I had no idea people could be that bad. It was the degeneration since WWII I guess.

They were brought up in a barn. Just one generation of feminist moms gave reason for alarm.

Americana was about independence of mind. But now it's all social, conformity, tyranny, aye!

30 years in desert seclusion and when coming back it was all social and their negative reactions.

Even the church acts as though the social is the way to salvation having been invaded by leftism.

THE STIGMATIZED/EVERYONE KNOWS

Anyone who's stigmatized is always on display while the others just fade in, hidden & happy.

The stigmatized feels shame thinking. "no one's as bad as me" when it's just perception see.

FLYING MONKEYS AND THE PRINCESS

The stigmatized are spotlit in that moment but as time goes on it's all reversed or forgotten.

"You can't believe how they all hurt me" cuz you were in the spotlight see--it's just groupthink.

Then if you rise up the group rejects each other, never talking again about the matter.

When stigmatized all your sins are illuminated whereas they get off Scot free tho' sinful/addicted.

Let specific people go and see it all as a herd. These are patterns seen across time/the world.

Until you see it as a system and human pattern you'll have grudges against specific relations.

You sin, you're handed over to the enemy. One way or another your power's depleted/no energy.

Due to their conditioned threshold limits they exploded calling you a lunatic but now forget it.

FLYING MONKEYS

While always looking innocent they incited riots against me. It was like them getting hitmen see.

Monkeys are problems cuz narcissists are cowards not seeking to correct but to get back.

It scared me suddenly as her group came against me. It wasn't until years later I saw why see.

They never knew me it was all their projection or listening to Jezebel & all her opinions.

Go grey rock, don't fight back [could get violent], no contact, go forward fast, have a blast.

FLYING MONKEYS AND THE PRINCESS

Why couldn't I see then every single one of Jezebel's friends and family came against me?

I'm in my reward now, protection from all I described herein. The intricacies of human systems.

Don't keep going back DOWN into the past. Memories are like anchors to demons/low class.

Jezebel wants to punish you cuz she's jealous. That's all, don't lose self-esteem in the process.

Suddenly her friends showed up. An invading army to "talk to me" and make me adapt to a slut.

It's horrible to face projections of flying monkeys who don't know me but call me names see.

The worse flying monkeys are the old bitties who are always on the horn being catty honey.

THEY HAVE A STAFF TO ATTACK YOU

The narcissist/Jezebel has a staff trained to attack you and make you feel unworthy: flying monkeys.

Jezebel trains her staff to see her as your victim so you deserve to be punished by them.

You often see this in family dynamics: the joint view that one deserves to be punished.

When the opinion leaders of the tribe plant evil seeds about you they all try to take you down.

Protect yourself. Your family was all you knew and false views monkeys were giving you.

The group had an entire narrative built around you and it acts as a program: you believe them.

FLYING MONKEYS AND THE PRINCESS

You begin to overcompensate to change the group's mind about you--and then self-annihilate.

Jezebel's staff are all the John's she's slept with who are always on call for errands get it.

JEZEBEL'S PATHOLOGICAL ENVY

Jezebel has pathological envy of any other female so turns her entire staff against the poor girl.

I said "you don't even know me, why are you in my home insulting me?" Well, it was she.

You have serial bullies in the family who fight treacherously by using flying monkeys.

You feel abandonment when always trying to please these flying monkeys never appeased.

Anyone in the whole dam family has been tainted by the evil finks molding how they think.

Relocate and then ban em all. You don't need these feelings when one turns cold to conform.

You say NO to Jezebel's demands and in comes her monkeys to persuade you to do them.

My obstructions were two older sisters. I literally had to outlive em to get out of the trenches.

The narcissist wants you miserable and to crush you, that's just the way it goes--incredible.

They don't like you for whatever reason like you shine too bright. Jealousy prevails, that's right.

CLEAN OUT THE WHOLE CANCER

FLYING MONKEYS AND THE PRINCESS

You gotta clean out the whole cancer. Ban all therapists and lawyers of these traitors.

Just by having a different opinion it's in the best interests of egotists to take you down.

They're gonna do whatever they can of course and use other people to do their dirty work.

A home in a safe place behind a locked gate is my reward for coming through all this ok?

Social Psychology was all I was interested in because these intricate systems were so complex.

That wicked Jezebel demonizing you will not get her hands dirty, it's always by others see.

Why did her brother hate me? Why did her lover hate me? Well now I know, it's was all she.

PROOF YOU'RE CRAZY

Suppose the narrative is you're crazy. They'll provoke you to be that way--see your history.

They called me crazy, I went crazy lashing out how I wasn't crazy and the group noted that see.

The flying monkeys aren't sent out directly but by planting seeds harvested eventually.

A flying monkey has been given little packets of info subtly, indirectly, suggested slyly.

They aren't sent out like hit men but picking up on the grapevine narrative and it happens.

Who are these flying monkeys? Some are narcissists, some love drama, some naive as hell.

FLYING MONKEYS AND THE PRINCESS

These sidekicks never take the time to see both sides of the story, they're raring to go see.

They only believe the victim narrative of the original narcissist & it's you they want to punish.

If a target of flying monkeys you're bombarded with projections contrary to who you are.

They have no basis in reality--these attacks mean you're are the opposite to what they say.

Monkeys always come into play cuz narcissists always move in packs coming to your house.

They've set things up so they are not the ones who are doing the abuse. Those are the rules.

THEY WANNA APPEAR INNOCENT

Abuse by proxy means she's not culpable--deniability which is believable--but you know that girl.

"I didn't do that, I'm sweet and loving" then the trauma bond continues with you begging.

If attacked by a group not directly by the narcissist he can twist it to look innocent--see this.

So you're left with no one to blame and only attacks by flying monkeys. Knowledge here is key.

In The Wizard of Oz the flying monkeys were sent to "GET HER" [Dorothy] and it can mean war.

Those close to the narcissist naturally seek to protect em so come against you without reason.

The monkeys are unaware they are being used by a narcissist to harm someone on their list.

FLYING MONKEYS AND THE PRINCESS

Until this happens personally you won't understand but when it does it's painful/sends you to bed.

A flying monkey can be a triangulation--anyone attached to another in your situation.

If a third actor starts acting funny you know something's up again: monkey persecution.

Flying monkeys cause incredible damage. They're like hit men unconstrained by tenderness.

You can't just blow em off cuz they know nothing about you because their damage is real.

They can ruin your reputation and dissolve your family who believes this false information.

Other people see the bullying and ostracizing of others bringing you down and they chime in.

To reject and ostracize you further from society is the goal of flying monkeys so stay alert honey.

Flying monkeys do great damage to you as a person. They do a job, unrestrained by reason.

It hurts to be attacked by a flying monkey group who all have the same narrative about YOU.

It's like they have a book which reads "this woman is this, this, and this" sung by a choir.

When they attack you don't fight back . Never try to prove yourself, go grey rock/no contact.

Live your best life, the greatest revenge is just living well. It hurts but that's the answer girl.

Get clarity, hit the Psalms mond stay with people who are loving, kind and see YOU for who you are.

JEZEBEL GETS AN ARMY AGAINST YOU

What I learned from a woman I knew: Never befriend a slut cuz a Jezebel will attack you with her male club.

She has low self-esteem already so will build a monkey army inevitably to go against what she ENVIES.

Jezebel uses "her men" as sidekicks or her army. She nurtures these relationships, so be ready.

If you know what you're dealing with you just say "wow they gave me a test to see if I'll agree--I will NOT.

If it's suddenly disappointing, discordant, divisive, fearful or painful SEVER this relationship then stay mindful.

KNOWING it's just a test for their narcissistic supply or to groom you, you can just joyfully cut it loose.

If they've been lovebombing then do something outlandish, shut it down or pay later. Jenna Ryan

If people are testing to see what level of disrespect you will tolerate, shut em down. The world is full of em.

The shit test is to ensure you're grade A supply. He wants total subservience to whatever he needs today.

The test shows whether you'll put up with their antics and be totally controllable. Go under or be a notable.

They're testing to see if you will be INSECURE enough and FOOLABLE enough to put up with their crap.

Any relationship with a narcissist will be filled with fear and apprehension of what they'll do to test you next.

You're superior to them, you see--throwing a wrench into your life is their only way to compete: see this.

THE VICTIM MENTALITY

The Victim Mentality of the narcissist is central here--that's why they make an army against you forever.

Narc being victim is strange too--since he does so many cruel and unpredictable things to you/his mule.

They play VICTIM since they can't take responsibility for what they do to others--it's automatic, built-in.

They gaslight the true victim by playing the victim. This is so damaging to the former and I can attest to this.

Gaslighting is damaging cuz it's all false accusation and calumny--ruining another person's reputation.

Reverse victimization says: Look what you made me do, whipping you.

After putting so much abuse on others, the way he sleeps at night is by playing poor-me who's married to her.

JEALOUS JEZEBEL'S COMPELLED TO GOSSIP

Jezebel is so jealous she's compelled to gossip so for example suddenly her friends will hatecha.

Why you little prickster! If you wouldn't say it to a child you shouldn't say it to a lady Mister.

Everything's going great in the relationship then suddenly they pull a giant test on you: avoid toxic people.

When the frenemy tests you it's a BIG THING. They let your dog out/bring evil friends over/it stinks.

The painful test makes you angry--so angry you can spit. This is YOUR test of the unequally yoked: REJECT.

FLYING MONKEYS AND THE PRINCESS

The minute you get that test you gotta close the door or they get comfortable disrespecting you more.

TAKES TWO FOR TANGO

If you tango with someone who trips you on purpose then you are going to pay. Jenna Ryan

If they don't ever email back why on earth would you confide in em when they finally decide to chat?

Pick up on immediate signs or be resigned to continued disrespect and abusers crossing your lines.

If he does something outlandish realize you're being tested and groomed to be narcissistic supply. Jenna Ryan

So that first test is the beginning of the sweet-mean cycle which I'm sure we're all familiar with in people!

She acts like your friend but brings hate to you from her men cuz she gossips jealously putting you down.

You must love yourself enough to cut-off this hideous monster even if temporary--never forget it Missy.

If someone blows up at you never see em again. These are tests of intimidation--pass em or go into destruction.

SIGNS OF INCREASING DISRESPECT

If they stand you up and don't bother to call: this should be a most obvious sign of disrespect--let em go.

It's not enough for them to disappear for two weeks while you cool down. People make mistakes, but so what?

People who give you this test--this excruciating, painful, expensive or sad test--are OUT, then forget em.

FLYING MONKEYS AND THE PRINCESS

This "test" will be an obvious break from what is normal--acceptable--in human interaction so be ready man.

WHY is it so obvious? Because it's designed to test you--whether consciously or not it's the jerk/shrew.

First she's your "friend" just borrowing, then to test she brings a hatchet-murderer into your house, see?

I don't need any more of these shocks from frenemies so the minute I sense em now I avert these tragedies.

NO SEX WITH YOUR EX

No sex with your ex. You don't wanna get attached when he's just gonna leave again, heck.

Thru sex you open old wounds so **NO SEX WITH YOUR EX** or you'll be withdrawing all over again.

A desire to please: all addictions are a result of unmet childhood development needs.

THEY DON'T KNOW HOW TO ACT

These people don't know how to act because the home's been broken for three generations: fact.

If you're one of those puttin' up with stuff are you ready to be **TOTALLY** disrespected as it progresses--huh?

Will you put the narcissist's needs ahead of your own, subjugating yourself, your dignity and your home?

These immature imbeciles are seeing what sticks--they're testing how far they can go to get their needs met.

We're both available if we need each other, otherwise we're alone and that's how we both need it in our home.

FLYING MONKEYS AND THE PRINCESS

If you don't face it now you're gonna face it down the road [with **BIGGER** tests] and if not then, you **WILL** face it.

Because the narcissist can also be a cruel sadist--that's part of his test. Nip it in the bud, cut it all loose.

When you see the flags, face it so you don't hurt when they go into **DEVALUATION** phase [brace for it].

If Jezebel's too weak to devalue you to your face she'll play nice and tear you down to her men: **FENCE UP.**

NARCISSISTIC SHIT-TESTS

The outlandish shit test happens **DURING** lovebombing stage then into devaluation. See the progression.

The poop-on-you test is specifically designed to see if you will be groomed properly for his narcissistic supply.

If you fail his test he'll move on. It means you have boundaries, self-worth, hope for the future--strong.

When you had the love thing going and suddenly there is cognitive dissonance, that's what I mean.

I couldn't believe it baby. Everything was so great then you pulled this test on me and what a tragedy.

It's enough to make us fuming angry. It's enough to make us **EXTREMELY** mad--It's a big thing this test we had.

You must close the door the minute you get that test--or that door is open to your valuables. Jenna Ryan

Get the signs straight--expecting a test, sweet to mean as they go to devaluation--or die a painful death.

Cuz if they're lovebombing then suddenly devaluing or getting mean, it can be terrifying--so see signs.

FLYING MONKEYS AND THE PRINCESS

Being part of these shit tests puts them above you--it gives them power over you. Cut them loose, and soon.

Look out for the shit test for it WILL come if you're dealing with a narcissist.

LOVEBOMBING THEN DISCARD

Idealization. Devaluation. Discard. These are the phases of the narcissist and don't forget his "tests" .

They start out wonderful, lovebombing you then it's **DEVALUATION** and things are never the same.

If unaware you spring into retrieval behaviors--doing anything to resume lovebombing but its no more.

The therapy is understanding the devaluation and discard phases--we're released from consciousness raised.

It's the difference between vampires and humans. They don't have our feelings, tho' they pretend to em.

I had to learn two things: I could not assume everyone was like me, and I don't have to like anyone.

What the liberal loser must get clear in her head is that there is **EVIL** out there. She's unfenced, laid bare.

You must close the gate: realize these people aren't conscientious like you-- seeking to destroy you too.

ABUSING OUR HOSPITALITY

We were taught to be kind and respectful but narcissists use this against us-- we must see this to resist.
By going **NO CONTACT** the narcissist can't get in. It instantly cancels his tests/games--do it now friend.

They don't care if you hate em, they just want your attention. Going no-contact eliminates anger.

FLYING MONKEYS AND THE PRINCESS

Stop thinking everyone is nice like you are. They are who they are and most are evil whether it's your sister/brother.

A narcissist has an innate inability to love and appreciate--and they are exploitational. It just is, pal.

It may be hard for you to understand your own flesh and blood just don't give a crap about you. Jenna Ryan

They're using your weakness--your need to feel loved and appreciated--and taking you over, don't allow this.

Remember, the narcissist is **NOT** nourishing tho' he says he is. You need to stay away/fill your life with thrills.

Narcissists may seem NICE. So we think: if only I hadn't done this/that, if only I was nicer/looked better.

You'll let him back in unless you block him internally. Let the fantasy die--it's a traumatic bond of misery.

LOVE BOMBING IS HEART NUMBING

He love bombs then blows hot and cold, pulls back. These are the insidious hurties that keep you a sad sack.

His mixed signals combine with thrilling hormones to create chaos inside--no contact will make it all subside.

The narcissist wants to give you just enough to keep you on a string--frazzled, messed up, dreaming of them.

They go cold and you want them to put back on their mask but they never will so you must go No Contact.

Grieve him like a death: mourn the loss of the fantasy of who you thought they were and regain Self.

Grieve the loss of your fantasy buttons--this guy got you goin' but he's never coming back, bet on it.

THEY HATE YOUR SUCCESS

They want to prevent you from succeeding/tear down everything you do. No Contact is the answer for you.

Lock the gate and protect your inner child. You'll feel so much better soon happy, protected and mild.

It's the family of origin that's imprinted a feeling of unworthiness, making you supply for the narcissist.

Narcissist wants you to feel faulty about everything you do then you realize you felt this your whole life too.

The silent treatment is their device of put-down. They're too busy for you, you're not worth it, a clown.

Narcissism makes you blue: They don't have time for you, you're not worthy of a return phone call, just stew.

Man's capacities prove we're not all one. Every species has its phenotype and true genius is ours in sum.

They're too busy for you, don't have time for you, you're not worthy--go into people pleasing mode quickly.

PATHOLOGICAL ENVY

The narcissist is pathologically envious and does not want you to succeed. You can't live your best life, see?

The narc wants you to feel foolish, stupid and unattractive. He just knows better so puts you in your place Sis.

They want you ostracized so post pics with others where you're not included or with women who are cuter.

They want you to feel optional or second fiddle. They want you to be an option--one among many who will do.

FLYING MONKEYS AND THE PRINCESS

Any type of a relationship with a narc will make you feel worthless, bad and faulty cuz they're superior see.

They can only deal with you in the role they require—docile, no self—cuz your True Self is their enemy no doubt.

If they're takers mirroring in you something you are **NOT**, become aware of their rot and put boundaries up.

Say: I am **AWARE** he's giving me the silent treatment making me feel worthless **BUT** this is not reality.

These people **CAN'T** respond to you because they are rancid meat and need you down to feel complete.

Free of rancidity you'll have responders to you, cutie. It's called reciprocity which now you'll have readily.

Never forget the narcissist enjoys hurting you cuz he's a sadist. That's the main thrill he gets, so resist!

HE JUST WANTS SUPPLY

You've gotta study narcissism especially if you're an empath, a decent/sensitive and good person.

They're only looking for **SUPPLY** and when childish tactics don't work they will **PERSIST** so you must **RESIST**.

After devaluing and discarding you they will usually circle around one more time, so be **READY** to stay sublime.

Get it thru your head that these are **NOT** like you. They are **NOT** decent or harmless but ravenous wolves.

To protect yourself take on the attitude of a war veteran or a cop. They've seen it all and know the scoop.

This guy is plastic and phony with a shiny exterior knowing just what to say to get fans/donations today.

Don't trust him. Learn to see thru the glitter and glamor cuz you've been this way before, it was war.

Learn from all the pain in the past that people have caused. Once you're hooked in it was nothing but hurt/stress.

GETTING DRUNK AT PEOPLE

You can no longer afford the health hazards of getting drunk at people so learn about evil to avoid it all.

All you must do is become **AWARE** by reading these words then **NO CONTACT** cuz that's how powerful it is girls.

I've been down this road, I know about the narcissist. He'll never give you credit and doesn't want your success.

If someone's shown dangerous/angry tendencies then trouble's right around the corner: think please.

The thing about unstable people is you don't see the signs until it's too late. Suddenly, you're **REALLY** irate.

Women didn't discard you, they just did it before you surely woulda done it to them as you've done to others too.

Why would I give up my castle running like a Swiss watch to live in your trailer with you, the debauched?

It makes me sick adapting to you and your routines. Mine took a lifetime, they're perfect it seems.

He doubts you--he needs proof! That's not a friend , he'd shout your sins from the top of the roof.

ENTITLED, GRANDIOSE AND CAN'T CHANGE

For the narcissist, forgiveness is permission. They aren't grateful for it, it just stirs em on to do it again.

FLYING MONKEYS AND THE PRINCESS

A "Christian" who cowers before men and won't state the truth just so he won't be rejected on Facebook?

You will never be enough for the narcissist--supply is like air and for a cheater it's everywhere.

How to stop seeking nurture from the betrayal source. This is the answer to a whole new life/new course.

What is toxic/constant shame? A sign that childhood dependency needs weren't met: nurture, affection.

When these core needs aren't met we take the blame and are infiltrated with toxic shame--that explains.

Toxic shame isn't healthy--it's not yours, it's "toxic". It's from something done TO you--shame "fixes it".

It's not normal shame, not your shame and maybe not even your parents but it's passed down just the same.

UNMET CORE NEEDS

When these core needs aren't met there is disassociation from yourself, self-disgust, separation.

No one paid any attention to me and my sisters insulted and degraded me constantly--I know this sad story.

Not only did they insult me they destroyed my rep [CALUMNY] and scapegoated: isolated me.

So I grew up alone in a bubble of shame and self-disgust and as time went on it got worse then I blew up.

My blow up was followed by total self-imposed solitary confinement in a cabin on 1000 acres of wilderness.

In isolation under the sun and stars I unraveled to the core and was put back on the potter's wheel by the Lord.

FLYING MONKEYS AND THE PRINCESS

I know what it's like to be ignored, brushed aside/walked by, minimized, hated by the gossiping horde.

SHAME FROM SEPARATION

SHAME biologically indicates separation from the pack or them rejecting you cuz you're old or sick.

Because of the crazy viewpoints from college brought home by liberal sisters mom drank herself to death.

She was told: If you wanna maintain relationship with us you gotta accept all this! She drank/didn't resist.

So they all got drunk together: folie a famille. A solidly Christian family was subsumed by a Hindu, see?

Suddenly alien elements entered our family. They are interlopers but if weak the system changes speedily.

I didn't fit their progressive liberal utopian viewpoint so I was cast out in shame though God did anoint.

I keep saying "it's over, it's done" but PTSD makes memories re-appear tho' I'm not that little girl.

STATE-DEPENDENT MEMORY

Just like an abused dog, consciousness flip-flops depending on what era you're in--Mom/now.

Hindu's laboratory abuse of animals put me in shock and depression for decades--this was my family?

Every culture's different dammit and that's all I'll say about it. How could sis marry that man/stomach it?

Tho' I'm behind a locked gate, safe--I feel imposed upon like hordes are at the door about to make me pay.

FLYING MONKEYS AND THE PRINCESS

I didn't get this way from some freak accident but from the social generation affecting everyone in it.

They acted like I didn't have a right to vet who comes in. Like everyone's my friend, I should be loving.

After years of self work, I don't ache anymore for people who are bad for me. Jenna Ryan

You've gotta guard the little girl inside--be there for yourself. Remember how it felt, no self-disgust.

Don't forget: If he shouldn't say it to a child he shouldn't say to a lady too--keep your mind/heart pure.

SELF-GROWTH OR SELF-SABOTAGE

It wasn't love or attraction--it was your usual projection of unmet needs onto a third party, man.

The answer to these unmet needs is to start focusing on yourself and your world--build it all up, girl.

Self-growth is easier than falling under the bus and going after someone who can't give us what we need.

Loving someone to our detriment is not love, it's sickness--masochism rooted and reduplicated from childhood.

It's not real love and it's not even a need. It's a blocked trauma that 's reaching out desperately.

Gotta work on this yourself otherwise you're stuck in Repetition Compulsion until the cycle's done.

Unmet needs when we're little means we're not enough and we must get it externally, thus this battle.

BECAUSE we're on repeat, we don't seek love from those who can give it but the same old apathetic spirit.

If you can't let go of someone it means you've unmet needs from childhood with a pattern of picking bad/not good.

26 years in desert wilderness all alone wiped out previous introjects and men I'd known--I just loved God.

The only time to meet those needs was early, not now. No false repeats, go back and love your child--WOW!

I felt imposed on by all men: told how to think, subtly degraded or mocked cuz I was different from most.

HURT OR RELOCATE/REJECT TEMPLATE

If you can't love your Self since no one else did, it doesn't get better from here--you MUST my dear.

It's a funny thing but usually if we can't let go of em, they weren't good for us: amoral psychopath, narcissist.

One psychopath I knew rejected Christianity and took up Eastern religions--he thought he was so good, man.

You're not hangin' on to a man/woman but something you needed and never got/they reminded you of that.

As he pulled away he wanted to sadistically make me pay so would intermittently come-here-go-away.

At that point I had to relocate. That's how strong this memory of the early trauma was--my template.

It was the same thing as early trauma: Among many others I was just one, nothing special here, movin' on.

TRIGGERED GAMES AND SHAMES

To play these games, to have these early anxieties of being NOT ENOUGH triggered is never, ever worth it.

FLYING MONKEYS AND THE PRINCESS

A true survivor would never go thru that again. Of playing second fiddle just so he can feel superior/no friend.

We develop internal working models of relationships early--it's a **TEMPLATE** and if unresolved is deadly.

Meet these issues head-on or repeat old templates--they don't change just cuz we became adults.

Yes, you were **IMPRINTED** towards a rejecting type of person. Someone who didn't want you, again.

Like a baby duck following its rejecting mother, you're gonna go for those minimizers and bluffers.

The answer is to build good neuropathways for the first time. Love your baby pictures as sublime.

You can't get over Frank if you're idealizing him. You've gotta see the substitution before it creates Bedlam.

You ran after people at two who pushed you away and you're pining for those who are indifferent today.

UNHOOK WORTH FROM REJECTOR

Unhook your worth from the rejector then you can let go and stop thinking about em. End of problem.

Don't you dare let your dignity be a doormat for things like that--the things he says cuz he's really a cad.

Not only is he **NOT** those qualities you're projecting, but those qualities are **YOURS**--think about the irony.

If you can't let go, 100% chance you're a codependent and he's a narcissist and this is just classic.

Usually this kind of misplaced hangup indicates arrested development--you got stuck in that strata.

People around you are a reflection of what you're needing. The next question is: why'd you let em in?

The Letting God must happen within me. Hating the other just maintains the endless bother of an inner tragedy.

Allowing someone to determine her reality chips away at her identity as she becomes the black widow spider.

Purely from childish unmet needs you put THIS person on a pedestal and idolized him--don't do this, please!

What ended constant emptiness was meeting ME--THE ONE--who was hurting after abandoning the self.

Take your eyes off narcissist and put it back on YOU where it belongs--cuz you needed him, crazy as it sounds.

When your cognition [you're not worth it] combines with inner beliefs [you're not worth it] = you've had it.

If that guy can't see right away that you're worthy and deserve respect, he doesn't care--now you reject.

You cannot change them and you cannot prove yourself to them. Even with riches and fame they'd disattend.

DRILL DOWN: WHAT A FIND

Two quick remedies on your way to the core: face that your parents weren't ok and that you must mourn.

As you drill down, how much you hurt is how much you NEED to since that uncracks/gets this thing going.

I hankered over him for years—no, decades. Thinking it was him when it was all about my templates.

There's a positive side to this bad start: many become over-achievers and hit the highest selling charts.

FLYING MONKEYS AND THE PRINCESS

It was a major trauma to a two-year old blocked at that level and who can never work it thru/repeats too.

RECAP: It wasn't him/her, it was your unmet needs from childhood causing you to cling, feeling insecure.

It's exhausting even to THINK of going thru it again. Round and round, up and down, confused, distraught.

Shamed, blamed, misunderstood, depressed from their black cloud, imposed on, too weak for objection.

It was from people my inferiors but since I was fallen that sort of thing doesn't apply anymore.

The Fallen Hero is killed by his supporters from before. Once you slip, watch out--here come the hordes.

You seemed to mirror me at first and it was refreshing someone understood but then it changed again.

The man most likely to chip away at her unique identity is the narcissist and becoming aware is her remedy.

NARCISSISM AND AGING BABIES

Why so much on narcissism suddenly? It's about aging babies--an entire generation like you don't wanna be.

Man loves his sins and will do anything to maintain em until hitting bottom and it all turns around.

Until hitting bottom--on the way down--they act like aging babies and this includes most all of us, sad to say.

Not until you know how much you can lose, and how fast you can lose it, do you become an adult/mentally fit.

The kids of the nouveau riche are complacent and that leads to dissipation cuz they feel invincible.

I had to lose everything and live on a shoestring to learn the most important things, it's about priorities.

To learn simplicity and essentially I had to live in a tiny cabin then took only those few things to a mansion.

Then when I humbled myself [was humiliated] enough God gave me all and I moved on up--like a miracle.

But the aging baby must learn a few things first. He has to undo every darn thing he's learned in this era.

Attraction, learn to take a step back. Attraction is just animal instinct but logic/reason is what we want.

Not appreciating the value of home until they're in a situation where they see it shelters em from harm.

I split a 5" pizza with two dogs and we're all on high energy, buzzing around getting it all done.

IT WAS SATAN NOT YOU

Stop feeling remorse about when Satan had control. Anything can happen, everything did, so what.

A change of diet can change all hormones and psychology [personality] instantaneously and amazingly.

No matter what you did it's still just a demon, the NOT-YOU. I know it's hard to forget it though.

Forget Politix! My new life is music or movies as we spiral down or rise up and hopefully face our enemies.

You wouldn't talk that way to a child and a lady's no different. It was disgusting now that I think of it.

It's not that I'm choking by not acting, but because I have great patience I believe in going slow/waiting.

FLYING MONKEYS AND THE PRINCESS

I'm not choking I'm waiting on God's direction honey.

Once the hero begins to spiral down in sin there comes a point where he can't stop--God hands him over son.

You deserve to have a life even though you screwed up. Thru' Jesus you get fresh start, clean slate, unstuck.

I'm not choking just contemplating: do I want to be seen? Anonymity is keen.

Freedom's why I'm here behind a wall and a gate and why I did everything to escape California a police state.

EVERYONE'S AN APOSTLE

In the world of religion now everyone's an apostle. But we're reviled, persecuted, defamed, made filth.

The true apostles were destitute but we follow and think the prosperity preachers are cute.

People send em money by the millions. They don't read the letters but the people are hypnotized by them.

The new breed is saying "who needs stuffy doctrines/ bible preaching?" Cuz if not, you don't have anything.

I'm not a preacher these are hymn lyrics and nursery rhymes.

When you admire Hollywood supermodels pretending to be religious you're giving into demons/feeling/emotion.

Prosperity teachers are here to destroy souls leading money-hungry people to a devil's hell.

They teach getting rich is magic by giving them money to get the job done. But we go directly to the throne.

You don't need a prosperity preacher [PP] you need Jesus Christ.

We are at the very last part of the church age.

FLYING MONKEYS AND THE PRINCESS

Enemies of the cross of Christ who's god is their belly, glory is their shame and who mind earthly things.

REBELLION IS WITCHCRAFT

Rebellion against God's word is counted as witchcraft. They pierce themselves thru with many sorrows.

If you're not cold nor hot--lukewarm--God'll spew you outa His mouth. He doesn't want anything to do with ya.

All thru history when women felt called to preach they started new religions that weren't biblical, see?

Women are not to have spiritual authority over a man and when it's children they turn out even worse than.

"I fell out of love". No you didn't, you chose not to love your wife. It's a CHOICE or there's constant strife.

If they aren't diligent and creative themselves they'll blame you for neglecting them--they aren't busy elves.

I've had losers/couch potatoes get angry, even violent with me because I rejected/disinvited them supposedly.

They don't do anything with their time and sleep in. It's just disgustin' so don't have anything to do with em.

I didn't put em up there to sell em--that's not how I make a livin'. They're my only legacy to those left standin'.

FEARING ENGULFMENT

After a certain age one fears engulfment or loss of identity. It's happened, so put things back on simmer, see?

Fearing engulfment by a bottomless pit or a deep cavern: that's the feeling in an experienced older person.

FLYING MONKEYS AND THE PRINCESS

It takes you down a rabbit hole and you don't know what they're gonna do--hurt again by a jerk/a shrew.

Feeling imposed on: like they wanted a piece of me--that's how I instantly felt, please let me be!

The minute I was around em they eyed me like a hungry tiger, searching me out, what can I get from her?

The women were equally bad--all wanting something or borrowing. I just hate that, I want solitude honey.

SOCIAL COMMUNIST SPIRIT COMES FIRST

In any room space I feel encroached upon by rapacious amoral youth but you were in your fifties, dude.

They don't know a thing but they want what you have. It's a sucking spirit, whether they need it or not.

They come into your house and outright ask: can I have this, can I have that? These are children, brats.

And it's all due to the communist spirit taught in the schools: they deserve it cuz you got more, fools.

Like a very young child, they come into your house and want everything. They want your life/fantasy.

They come into your home and bring their friends without asking. You don't get a chance to vet--that's hating.

The Social comes first so if you don't accept ruffians you're a hater and being asocial is an "anxiety disorder".

So the communist spirit allows them to take your things and bring their friends--we're all one, earthlings.

If you don't like "MY FRIENDS" you're a hater and this could be a violence-inciter. Watch, beware!

SIMILITUDE IN GENERATIONS

Since they're all cut from the same cloth they go along with those things which you despise and are abhorrent.

Porn addiction is all about withdrawn attention. Life is a pie and you just became a much smaller piece.

It took a lifetime to realize I even needed a wall and a locked gate. I was naive and loving: bad fate.

There is similitude to each generation. That's the bell-shaped curve, the herd, social acculturation.

It may spread to homosexuality from porn. It makes sense that it would generalize--no lines about a thing.

A continual dropping on a rainy day and a contentious woman are alike. Prov 27: 15. Drip, drip, drip.

Women shouldn't talk to other women's husbands because this is the setup for affairs, you've seen em.

Woman should stay in the home to prevent this or stay with women--except then the divorcees influence em.

A woman should obey her husband not take instructions from another man cuz that triggers her emotions.

Don't remorse over wasted years. Life is short, suddenly it's over so with all your heart love the Lord.

One little word, one raised eyebrow, looking at a woman a little too long--its all it takes/she's back in his face.

I was banned by the feminist moderator for the most obtuse, obscure, far-fetched, ridiculous reason.

Investigative behaviors triggered by betrayal trauma ARE our mal-adaptive illness but so what, we gotta do it.

FLYING MONKEYS AND THE PRINCESS

Not a wizard I've just done my homework.

DEMON TRANSMISSION

They were crazy and their demons got on you and then you became even worse and then it ran it's course.

How could Paris Syndrome be a mental illness when Paris really IS filled with violence, trash and rudeness?

Betrayed wives are always so happy when things are stable and predictable. But then, outa the blue....

A big change is coming--remember whether good or bad change causes stress: mind your diet/sleeping.

I believe in terseness and laconic alacrity so don't write long letters and don't over-explain--spit it out, ok?

TO BEWITCH

To "bewitch" is to fascinate and charm in a misleading way. That's your guy, a new trinket or the church today.

Social engines just turn off your counter so you don't know who's looking and they aren't getting em either.

Intense attractions and feelings: watch these! Take control, don't be the victim of alluring sirens.

For that alluring siren that's exploding in your attractions may turn out to be an illusion for your destruction.

Never interrupt your enemy when they're destroying themselves. Napoleon Bonaparte

I don't like things that are bigger than I am--like I'm swooped up. I'm pulled by God, He fills my cup.

I can't allow myself to be swept off my feet by you. I will fight this thing because self-control is a fruit.

FLYING MONKEYS AND THE PRINCESS

I declare this to the whole world: You **WILL** not do this to me, I will take control because now I am whole.

I will fight these feelings and emotions to the end because I've learned they're not my friend/I'll ignore em.

PULLED, NOW SWEPT UP

We wanna be **PULLED** by God not **SWEPT UP**--off our feet, down another street, the self depleted, effete.

I can hear someone yelling/screaming at me inside. That's an introject--swallowed whole tho' they died.

The YMCA now says that white people are racist and you should give them money to fix this.

Is this really logical to you? NO. Then why are you going along with this cruel, silly nihilistic worldview?

White Europeans believe in individualism--non-racism. But all non-white cultures are deeply racist, ALL of em.

Instead of complaining about the ruffian ask yourself why the hell you let him in, and why you needed him!

Crushing grief, heart cracking open, unraveling and rebirth after your relationship ends. Alan Robarge

Not-doing is just as much doing. Acting brashly or prematurely is untimely and foolish.

I will WAIT till God gives me that cue cuz I know it'll fall together in a fabric and a whole new view.

The dems are giving up their opportunity to be an equal partner in leadership just cuza partizan politix.

Pelosi will be remembered as the first to impeach a duly elected president simply on partisan politics.

There are no shoulds, there are only shalt nots--and the first one is to keep sinners out of your house.

DON'T BE A CHESHIRE CAT

Smiling like a Cheshire Cat in photos is a new phenomenon. See the old pics-- they're ALL solemn/no fakin'.

Smiling [say cheesecake] in photos is part of modern day fakery. Nowhere in old portraits do we see smilies.

It's getting so you can't do or say anything without bringing offense but that's ok, it clears the decks.

If seeing himself thru eyes of others he's hypersensitive to their moods. Need separation from these old bonds.

Gaslighting is also changing your reality so that you doubt yourself. If he's rigid and you're artistic it's hell.

Girl, if you're smart but without a solid sense of self you're gonna be gaslighted constantly--don't let it be.

GASLIGHTING THRU DEVALUING

Another form of gaslighting is devaluing you after they said you were great. It's a rudder of control: flattery.

The last form of gaslighting is unasked for advice. This is really insulting and a Jezebel brought him.

He got hot under the collar/his face turned red. He was mad but what had I done? That's gaslighting man.

His reality is superior to hers--that's the message of a gaslighter--and to make it worse he's miffed at her.

And he doesn't have the slightest idea why she does things. This is all projection cuz it's not like HIM.

He writes what he thinks from his ego or what he's heard. That's not true genius, he's part of the herd.

Solution for narcissist victims: Just think of the unparalleled humility of Jesus compared to him.

I elect to stay in the home, protected from ravenous wolves--only here do I feel safe as I should.

ROOTLESS IS CLUELESS

Some men wanna make you rootless so you fly away with them without any checks against em. Stay home!

They want you so rootless they insist you fly away in a MOMENT--yes that's what he said. Forget it.

As if a woman has NO roots even tho' we are the home creators, that's our suit. It's such an insult.

Women: NEVER give up your dog, horse or home for a man. This is happening all the time, it's so sad.

In reality they're not after me, they're after you--I'm just in the way. Donald Trump

FLUSH EM OUT. See who they really are. Lure them out with your pawn to win the entire game, see afar.

The biggest money makers on youtube are also the most boring. The IQ demography is so low it's showing.

You can make millions by eating mountains while talking about nothing and the herd eats it up, adoring.

The devil is 99% right or mostly true. It's that little lie amongst truths that marks the jerk or the shrew.

I searched him out and found the error but then he said the same about me and being his mirror brought anger.

FLYING MONKEYS AND THE PRINCESS

Butter, starch, sugar--all the bad things and I weigh 100 lbs. working 18 hour days and all night long I swear.

America on the brink with a deep stink started by liberal petulance over dead dogma, what they think.

You're so puerile and simple, this really isn't deep and eternal so I'll leave you to it, good luck lil' boy/girl.

NEVER LOWER STANDARDS TO FIT

So they're all dumbed--you think I'll lower my standards to force the fit to them? Bring em up instead.

It's up to God whether you get anything outa this--it's pulling power: good/bad discernments of the hour.

I see you, a puerile simpleton, criticizing me and I think: I begged for this due to temporary low self-esteem.

Charisma will get you there but your weakness in character won't keep you there.

There'll be seasons of chastisement, seasons of nothing going your way just so God can see how you'll act.

There's a lot God's got to do **TO** you before He can ever do anything **THROUGH** you. Joyce Meyer

To enforce tolerance they lock us up but we're only tolerant if allowing ourselves to be criticized and mocked.

The house impeached itself by perpetrating a fraud on the American people who voted for President Trump.

The average leftist is so dumb he thinks impeachment equals conviction and that's what they're sayin'

Christianity Today is another example of false/fallen religion who knows nothing and is just virtue signaling.

FLYING MONKEYS AND THE PRINCESS

It makes me sad to see a violinist become a mukbanger stuck in gluttony and sex perversions.

Facebook, Twitter and all social media banned Alex Jones on the same day. Simultaneously he was erased.

We the true Americans do not want to remove from office the architect of our prosperity.

NEPOTISM IS BAD, MAN

Nepotism isn't just about getting your relative a job! It's also about you going along with his sins/charades.

Nepotism is about you covering for your relative just cuz he is. That's why tribalism is so violent and insidious.

There's right and wrong whether its your relative or not! You covering for a sinner shows your own rot.

Why can't we just be friends? Why can't we get past this? Cuz you act like it never happened/doesn't exist.

He covers for his relatives cuz he doesn't know right vs. wrong anyway. Cultural decline sinks that way.

I went thru the tunnel to death then God brought me back with a Creative Act- -I write when cued: fact.

Just Stick to Things You Know: The answer to making sure you don't make an ass of yourself again.

Nikocado Avocado knows the more absurd, ridiculous, messy and debauched he is the more his fans grow.

Putting his total breakdowns of mental illness on video explodes his fanbase, and he has said so.

I've done my homework. It's established science put poetically comprising the Social Science paradigm.

SHIT-SHOTS TAKE ME DOWN A NOTCH

Your little shit-shots to take me down a notch are obvious to me so I'm gone Sarge/hit the road Jack.

Was it really worth you goin' out like that--with a cheap shit-shot just to establish dominance? Oh yah.

Women, talk only to your husbands. Ask NO man's advice cuz your emotions are triggered/you're pulled down.

Talking to a man other than your own husband may seem titillating but quickly becomes depressing.

You and spouse have a home, you've adapted. This other character's not part of that--he's way out/defective.

He's dirty so let him go--you have a home. Never take a chance of losing by another syndrome/episode.

I keep feeling like someone's gonna hit me. That's from years of mal-adaptation to users intimidating.

Once I learned everything necessary God wrenched me away from the desert wilderness after 31 years.

This is biology, not psychology. It has to do with the original imprint: if his mom was fat, he wants that.

Think: He's playing victim when I'm the victim but I'm gonna refocus on myself and forget the narcissist.

DISCARDING AFTER SEX—OUCH!

DISCARDING: One day you're important and I love you, the next day you don't exist--you've been ERASED.

They discard then put you in the trash. If they need you again they'll take you out, only to put you back.

FLYING MONKEYS AND THE PRINCESS

Discarding isn't a normal breakup. It's sudden, it's extreme and it's so very painful many may just give up.

The one discarded feels betrayed, abandoned and objectified: terror in the gut, confusion, minimized.

Your feelings are irrelevant. He can put you in the trash and take you out whenever he wants you nut.

He wants you when he wants you, he doesn't when he doesn't and that's all he's gonna say, now forget it.

I experienced this with one so inferior but by rejecting me with my templates I saw him as superior.

Now you see how twisted our relational world can be. It dates back, confuses facts, turns our world black.

We want this guy cuz we want resolution--CORRECTION--of the original trauma with [cold, drunk] momma.

EVERCHANGING FEELINGS

I don't want you now, may want you tomorrow. Your feelings are irrelevant or I'd treat ya like an angel.

Narcissistic mother creates not-good-enough daughter--not just criticizing constantly but SHAMING her.

If you talk about your feelings and emotions she'll discourage it, saying "you're just too sensitive".

She's accomplishment-oriented. If you make her look good, great--if not you're discarded as old freight.

Why complain of loneliness, dude? You're rid of those who victimized you, in a new life too, it's just an interlude.

I complained of pain being stuck in the past where lessons were gained and not realizing I'm super-ok today.

Those users/confusers/misusers/abusers are gone forever and I'm never going back to that level, ever.

I will **NEVER** let em in to my home unvetted again. I will never take this lightly, I've learned my lesson friend.

NARCISSIST MOTHERS

The alcoholic narcissist mother is secretly mean. At home she's downright nasty, cruel, even obscene.

The children of alcoholics were abandoned. So they fear abandonment and are attracted to it, doomed.

Instead of brooding over Jezebel who wrecked your life, thank God you're finally rid of her/out of strife.

You gravitate to the same old feud: they lack empathy, can't deal with emotions and ever-blaming you.

Instead of hankering for old crutches whom you didn't love that much, thank God you're rid of these blocks.

With emotional needs unmet as a child and not validated as a young girl there a hole inside that's never filled.

The emotional loneliness, the void, the hole inside making you feel you're undeserving or don't belong.

BEHAVIOR SHIFTS TO PEOPLE PLEASE

You're used to changing behavior to people-please. You believe you're to blame, not good enough, a sleaze.

So you take the blame, hoping that this time things will work and you'll finally get all the love you deserve.

What is that vacuum inside, that hole we're trying to fill with another sick relationship? Let's examine it.

Drill down to the beginning--ok mom wasn't loving. But she had other qualities we could be admiring.

As an adult you must become the mother you never had and nurture your damaged child called "bad".

Now you'll build your self-worth on what you've achieved--not social status/climbing, and what a relief!

When those self-critical thoughts come up, say "that's not true--that's mom talking" and they will stop.

Mom drank all day [loud brawls to see], shamed me publicly and sisters hated me--yet here I am today.

COLLATERAL DAMAGE: YOU

The collateral damage lasted decades because I didn't see these patterns but you can and quickly be happy.

Daughters of narc mothers: overachievement [I'll prove it to you] brings imposture syndrome [I don't deserve it tho'].

Daughter keeps working for more and more outer success cuz it's what mom wants but it never works.

Mother wants daughter's outer success--achievements--but takes no account for her character--who she is.

Frantic daughters of narcissistic mothers seek only for EXTERNAL validation that they are good enough.

COPING DEVICES: FOOD, DRUGS, SEX

Or she could just give up since she's never good enough and become a self-sabotager /underachiever.

The self-sabotager who is never-good-enough turns to alcohol, drugs and food addictions to fill that hole.

FLYING MONKEYS AND THE PRINCESS

These crutches she uses to turn her ANGER inwardly to destroy herself since her mother she can't kill.

I used food as a crutch to fill that angry sad hole which is why of my daily fasting routine I'm so proud.

As a bottomless pit for love needs unmet, the energy traveled to bio level: food for emotional survival.

So now your huge love needs means you never get enough food cuz all that [esp. bad] food makes you weak.

FOOD ADDICTION—WHAT ELSE IS THERE?

Some divorced women stick their head in the frig and never come out: unmet emotional needs/spiritual draught.

With every hurt real/imagined I thought of food. The brain instantly sought it's solution and it was cruel.

Vegan malnourishment made me more obsessed, adding fat satiated and I was rescued: God had blessed.

Ever since adding fat in 1990 I never craved food again. In fact, it's a chore to eat so I just get it over with.

Simultaneously my emotions healed. The shame was leaving, God was with me and He was my shield.

Recognize the cycle and that the dynamic with your narc mom was NOT healthy then forgive her today.

I never heard from you and never would've heard from you again so why would I leave you a nickel, friend?

Dynamic with narc mother did NOT meet your emotional needs and DOES affect the way you are as an adult.

Daughter sees herself as not good enough--despite her accomplishments she's a failure and it's rough.

FLYING MONKEYS AND THE PRINCESS

FILLING UP THE BLACK HOLE INSIDE

Recap: FILL THAT VOID NOW. Keep saying "I am good enough" and admire all you've accomplished—wow

By the way, you were always good enough--you just have to believe it: before this fall you were the princess.

Write down narc mom's best qualities. Write down yours. Now throw the whole negative bag out to dead history.

She hurt me, Dad and all of us. But she was just passing down the template and so it's easy forgiveness.

The fact she had to drink herself to death says much, she was hurting possibly more than all of us.

We naturally project stuff out and you were there, sitting on the couch. Now let it all go and enjoy your lunch.

They don't care about what's most important to God: sex sins. They only care if they "offend".

When I withdrew focus from the target it lost its charisma. That was MY unmet needs--I've learned that from Thee.

DRILLING DOWN BRINGS PANIC

When you drill down it brings panic at first--then you see mom didn't even like you but things coulda been worse.

44,000 quips and 106 books trying to get mom's approval. It never stops, that's how it works and it's brutal.

Mom died 30 years ago but that doesn't matter--the original template is the steam engine up the latter.

Even if she did know of my achievements would she even care? Before you drill down that far, prepare.

FLYING MONKEYS AND THE PRINCESS

And if she didn't care, so what? She fed me, protected me, kept me safe and warm--that's all we can want.

What were her good qualities? She was Mrs. La Mesa, she was a great hostess and she created a paradise.

What about me not being good enough? I look at what I've achieved, my routines/good habits, the pets I love.

FEELING YOU'RE REPLACEABLE

The gnawing feeling you're replaceable, dispensable, not that much at all-- won't ever occur again y'all.

If they walked you by, with success their outa your sight. Don't ever forget only time-tested trust is right.

I'm a psychologist--I study ABNORMAL psychology. We don't study healthy people ya know, that'd be boring.

The more you drill down to the original trauma--to work that out--the more crying jags will consume ya.

When I finally cried my last tear and accepted without fear [past and future] I was clear: colors everywhere.

It's good to know the reason for perpetual shame: Your mom didn't like you and played mental games.

The best way to get over narcissistic false brothers is to get into your own creativity which they'll have no part of.

Collaborators are sunk! Outline of what's to come. How wonderful: the revolution has begun.

The more creative you are the less you'll focus on that guy who devalues/minimizes you like you're NOT a star.

No one ever said he has to love or even read what I do. He keeps me afloat while I dream afar to a new view.

FLYING MONKEYS AND THE PRINCESS

He may not ever read it but believes in me who wrote it. It's only feminists who insists he do that but forget it.

PHONY FEMINISTS

It's only phony feminists who insist on being called "Dr." or "Reverend" or how about "Apostle" or "Prophetess".

Simplicity in your words--laconic terseness--shows guts and self-assurance and I have that for sure.

In contrast, liberal black women have it easy and can cash in. Grease the skids by keeping the narrative goin'.

But if you're a black conservative your career is over. Well not forever, God will get you in there somewhere.

Families breaking up over Trump: that's the level of psych warfare going on, targeting thru the media.

You gotta drill down to the core--the original trauma--and the closer you get the more crying's goin' on.

And then once you get there--seeing mom didn't like you, boo hoo--it all dissolves and everything's ok.

CHURCH INSIDERS

To be accepted in the inner circle you must be social and to be reclusive and eccentric is evil.

They begin to look alike--ordinary, rounded & bloated in loss of identity surrounded by frenemies.

Every herd has it's own threshhold limits beyond which novelty brings negative reactions.

In the social conformist era novelty [autonomy, independence] brings violence instantly.

FLYING MONKEYS AND THE PRINCESS

Having been violently reacted **TO** they bring the same fear-based learned reactions to **YOU**.

This was my Ph.D. in the Streets. To gain this wisdom escape culture for 30 years then tweet.

WEEKLY FASTING: CHURCH

Anorexia is complete debilitation from a combination of starvation and terror of your fellow man.

Eat once daily and fast one day a week totally. Stretch your fasting skills for that's your healing.

Realize each fasting day brings greater gains so you have so much to look forward to ok.

To be happier while fasting think of all the good you're accomplishing without doing a thing.

Fasting on Sundays is my church. If chemically sensitive [separated] you can still emerge.

Can't go around people cuz they make me sick. Anywhere humans are chemicals are thick.

Most can't skip even two meals. Do it: fast just one day that's all, an achievement that's real.

Prove to God that He comes before food--that you've an appetite for truth and holy solitude.

No chattering in the sanctuary! But I hear loud cackling, rock music, people talking.

The deacons are chosen for popularity and social connectivity not being godly/scholarly.

In get togethers all scramble to sit next to the king and queen of the social: a church low.

FLYING MONKEYS AND THE PRINCESS

They kept switching places to manipulate the most socially profitable sitting arrangement ok.

THE LEFTIST SOCIAL CHURCH

That isn't church. Being social is not a requirement for salvation but they act like it is, AMEN.

I felt sickened in my core at the social atmosphere so went into my room and found Him there.

To introverts church can be the most traumatic day of the week--freaked not being in the clique.

I found God in total solitude in the desert wilderness all alone in my little cabin with bible readin'.

I felt so good leaving Mr. and Mrs. Deacon Social Charm behind in love with the Divine.

It felt good to leave CLIQUES behind, so fascistic like they were superior in God's mind.

The socialization of church is exactly how it has fallen. God's disgusted as they keep addin'

CUM-BA-YAH CHURCHES

The socialized church is CUM-BA-YAH as even songs are made acceptable to liberal minds.

The worldly social church scared me and I'm sure I'm not the only one. Synagogues of Satan.

They add and subtract from the true gospel and it's shocking how they relabel good from evil.

Everyone clamors for attention from Mrs. Social Charm. She's seen as THE most holy and warm.

FLYING MONKEYS AND THE PRINCESS

Not the odd girl sitting in the back and so nondescript. She can't be holy, she's not the elect.

Church insiders, outsiders, cliques and popular divas: change your fate thru the psalms escape.

The millions of non-citizens flowing in should be able to choose our government: END GAME.

I feel young cuz age is appears a mix of infantilization, psychosis and higher consciousness.

As memory and body recedes allow the temporal lobes to explode to a panoramic view aglow.

Is it poor memory or ascendency to higher realms with different priorities? Let's rethink eldering.

Allow yourself to fall out of structure without excuses. Stop apologizing and just be sages/muses.

THEY SIDED AGAINST YOU

You were betrayed by your sisters, brothers, mothers and cousins. It's still all irrelevant son.

It's what we came here to learn: trust no man. Read the first paragraph of the Psalms friend.

THEY [the herd of grifters] GATHER TOGETHER to pull US down, the peculiar who love God.

I was sickened to my core at the social atmosphere so escaped to a ghost town & found Him there.

I hated being around peers since kindergarten. School phobia set in, I literally couldn't stand em.

The elder human is very interesting. Unique as he can be and valuable for just that reason see.

THEY HATE THE SUPERIOR MAN

Superior man must be ready for everybody trying to take him down. The more superior, the more they hate him.

What exactly did he do? Nothing, that's what. It's just like Trump.

Trump isn't the first president with a populist streak who makes uncomfortable entrenched elites.

What exactly did Nik do? NOTHING. Liberals are ALWAYS finding things to be offended at!

It's a sucking spirit compensating trauma: they want everything that is yours in America.

Hitler was a drifter living in Vienna then crowds fed his psychosis and he rose up as leader.

Sadistic brutality and strange customs are in their soul from when small, no discussions allowed.

Troops on the streets, paramilitary police and citizens ratting you out/getting in your face.

The gigantic Biden backlash: we all hate him now. The Afghanistan disaster is the last straw.

Anxieties about Afghanistan: the Taliban's harsh brand of Islamic justice and repression of women.

They tell me it's the white man I should fear but it's my own kind doing all the killing here. Tupac

They never complained with he was a pervert, they only did when he "offended"/brought someone to tears.

A 13 % anti-impeachment shift in Democrats is catastrophic for Pelosi and her minion rats.

FLYING MONKEYS AND THE PRINCESS

Pelosi's failure is of epic proportions and her political future is looking exceedingly grim at this point--for sure!

Nancy Pelosi launched impeachment to damage Trump for the 2020 election and she is failing spectacularly.

By impeaching Trump the Democrats INSURED his 2020 win and for that I can't thank you enough, friends!

Of course they want globalism--then they control everyone.

The more bad you feel about being white the more virtuous you think you are. How'd we get here? Jared Taylor

It's not shaved, it's 1/8" female buzzcut and I LOVE IT. The breeze, sun, wind and air feel so good with almost no-hair.

What about the lectins, oxalates and goitrogens in greens? I feel much better with none of it, I even eat cheese.

PERSONAL OBSERVATIONS

Cure for sick cat--she couldn't even walk! I petted her while she fasted three days and now she's well.

AGEISM is the worst objectification, beyond race. Seeing you through a number is like spitting in your face.

Never panic if your cat or dog stops eating. They are naturally fasting--celebrate their new beginning.

My cat stopped eating and wouldn't even drink water. No problem--she's her own doctor.

If we should follow food combining rules--splitting starch from fat--why have people never looked this bad?

The only answer to the bulge is eating one meal a day—even just two starts to build the bulky false body.

FLYING MONKEYS AND THE PRINCESS

They talk about absolutely nothing--just an aimless stream of logorrhea: these are the high paid mukbang youtubers.

The biggest money makers on youtube are also the most boring. The IQ demography is so low it's showing.

I can't go all fruit cuz I"m always hungry/low energy. I was brought up on dairy but just one meal, amazing.

Pizza gets the job done, that's all. It's for us workers and that means energy, creativity--make it habitual.

Buy bulk: dough balls, pizza sauce, pizza seasoning, cheese and pepperoni if you please. Easy

We have to eat right? So it's good to settle on something, get the elements in and agree to a good routine.

If I eat one nut later after breakfast, it's burp-burp-acid all day. ONE meal means ONE meal, "not a morsel".

EVERYTHING'S GOT SOY IN IT

Everything's got soy in it now, a cheap crop--who needs that crap? Gat caputo pizza dough, it's old type.

Only a fool thinks he can always do what he's always done. Joyce Meyer

Paleo is fruit, veg, nuts, meat. Take any of these then fast for long periods-- that most reflects man early.

If you wanna slip dairy into meat category, go ahead. The point is the fast after you've eaten, even bread.

My Dapper Dad died at 84 with still jet black hair and he lived on bread and butter--LOTSA the latter.

Even if you mess up, what the heck--clean the kitchen, fast for the day and start over again tomorrow, OK?

ONE DAY FAST A WEEK

The key to longevity is eating one meal a day but hey who'd do that but a narcissist like me?

The key to youthifying queenology is to eat once a day honey then all wrinkles will go away.

Carb up in the morning, fast for the day. Fast one day a week unfailingly and now you'll be ok.

Fast one day a week to keep everything sharp. You'll be amazed with energy off the chart.

Not only does a weekly fast correct the problem you're better than before the cycle started.

Fast first: It's the last test before success if you haven't done it yet or just promised it.

To open that matrix you gotta change something, shake things up, overcome the block.

The degree of early trauma determines extreme attachment to addiction compensating it.

It was a generational curse. That same demon bothered your great grandfather first.

Can you constrain appetite in respect to a principal? That's the test of knights/good people.

Remorse? Chalk it all up to a demon you had at that time and that's it [anything can happen}.

Stop fearing your future will reflect your past. Everything has changed, you'll have a blast.

Nothing can resist the human will that will stake its existence on its purpose. Ben Disraeli

The best talents ripen late, it took a lifetime to get to this point. Evolved skills with God's anoint.

100 KAREN KELLOCK BOOKS

AFFINITY OR MISERY
AGELESS CORNUCOPIA
AMERICA AWAKE!
AMERICA'S DAFT ERA
ARTS OF PALEO FASTING
AUTOPHAGY ON CHEATERS
BACKSTABBING NEUROTICS
BETRAYAL TRAUMA
BOOMERS AND BROKENNESS
BOOT ON NECK
CHAMPION GUIDES
COMMIE NUTHOUSE
COMMIES
COMMUNIST SPIRIT
CONTAGION OF MADNESS
CONTAGIOUS MADNESS
CULTURE CLASH BASHED
DAFT LEFT
DAILY FASTARIAN
DAM RATS
DIVERSITY IS CRUELTY
E-RACE WHITE
EVIL FREAKS (Beyond Gross)
THE END OR A BEND?
FEMALE BULLIES AND FEMI-NAZIS
FEMALE CARNALITY
FEMALE DUMB DOWN
FEMALE POWER DRIVE
FEMINISM AND RUIN 1 & 2
FIX FOR MISFITS
FOOLS & TRAMPS
FREEDOM SPEAKING
FRENEMY ENABLER
FRENEMY LIAR
FRENEMY THIEF
FRENEMY TRAITOR
TRENEMY TYRANT
GENIUS IS HELD DOWN
GLOBALISLAM
GOD USES THE FLAWED
HAZE OF THE LATTER DAYS

KAREN KELLOCK PH.D.

M.S. Political Science, San Diego State. Ph.D. in Psychology, University of California Irvine. Postdoctoral: UCI School of Medicine, Dept. of Psychiatry [NIMH Grants]. Developed the Debris Theory of Disease, a theory of system pathology in 120 books and 22 textbooks for the general public. The theory has a general formula: All disease is obstruction, all recovery is elimination, all success is attraction. The three obstructions are people, habit and food. Remove obstruction and snap to your goals, waiting in the wings.